Are you ready to have some fun?

Thank you so much for ordering the Pre-K YOUR Way Curriculum Series. I created these activities to support caring parents and teachers like you in creating meaningful learning experience for your children. I hope you enjoy these activities as much as I enjoyed creating them.

Please contact me with any questions or comments that you have while working through the curriculum booklet. I want to hear from **YOU!**

If you enjoy these activities, please write a review on the product that you purchased. All products can be found at:

www.jdeducational.com

Happy Playing, Learning and Growing!

Sincerely,

Jeana Kinne

DEDICATION

This Curriculum Series is dedicated to all parents and teachers striving to provide optimal learning opportunities for the children in their care. Thank you for your patience, love and support in nurturing little minds, creating a positive impact on our future generations.

DISCLAIMER

JDEducational and the author is not to be held responsible for injury or damage created or caused while preparing for or completing the activities in this book. Adult supervision, safety and caution should be used at all times. Do not leave children unattended while completing these activities.

Pre-K Your Way Activity Series

About Our Curriculum

Our Curriculum is designed to strengthen school readiness by meeting the identified skills and concepts, which are necessary for a smooth transition to Kindergarten. These curriculum modules include low-cost/no-cost activities which parents, preschool staff and home daycare providers can use with the children in their care.

This curriculum was developed using current Kindergarten Readiness Assessments including: Common Core Kindergarten Standards, the Preschool Learning Foundation and the Desired Results Developmental Profile.

This curriculum addresses the following areas of development:

- Cognitive Development
- Mathematical Development
- Physical Development
- Language Development
- Literacy Development
- Social-Emotional Development
- Self-Help Skill Development

This curriculum was developed to meet the interests of all children and based on the multiple intelligences theory by Howard Gardner. Gardner was a Harvard University Professor who believed that traditional education wasn't utilizing the strengths of all children. Every child is unique and learns differently. Gardner identified eight different "intelligences" and pathways to learning.

These eight intelligences include:

1. Linguistic – "word smart"
2. Logical-Mathematical –"numbers/reasoning smart"
3. Spatial - "picture smart"
4. Bodily-Kinesthetic – "movement smart"
5. Musical – "Rhythms and songs smart"
6. Interpersonal – "People smart"
7. Intrapersonal – "Self smart"
8. Naturalist – "outdoors/nature smart"

Learning Objectives - Level 2

These activities have been developed to meet specific, age-appropriate, Kindergarten-Readiness skills. These skills are laid out in the learning objectives of each activity. The following activities may be completed in any order desired and are specifically designed to address the academic domains: math, science, language, literacy, cognitive, problem solving, and social-emotional development. **After completing all modules in the Level 2 Curriculum Series, the child should be able to:**

Mathematics

- Identify objects by classification.
- Sort objects into categories by at least one attribute.
- Show understanding of measurement and begin to associate measurement descriptions (big, small, long, short).
- Recite numbers 1 through 10 in order.
- Count objects with one to one correspondence.
- Describe the similarities and differences of several shapes that include circle, triangle, square and rectangle.
- Create and finish simple patterns that include two elements.

Science/ Problem Solving Skills

- Develops solutions to a problem.
- Asks questions and performs simple investigations.
- Works through tasks that are difficult.
- Demonstrates understanding of visual and verbal prompts.

Language and Literacy

- Demonstrate the understanding that letters make words.
- Uses language to talk about past events.
- Uses words and increasing vocabulary to retell a story.
- Uses a variety of vocabulary to describe finding solutions to problems.
- Uses language in conversation to discover answers to questions.
- Follow simple two-step directions.

Gross Motor/Fine Motor Development

- Uses gross motor movement skills to access a variety of obstacles and environments.
- Hops on one foot, without support, three or more times.
- Runs and Jumps over small objects.
- Uses scissors appropriately.
- Uses a crayon or pencil to draw or write.

Table of Contents

Each unit builds on concepts learned in the previous unit.
Activities within each unity may be completed in any order desired.

Setting up an Indoor Learning Environment at Home

Home-based learning environments tend to be one of the most complicated and multi-functional spaces in a home. Not only do parents need to make room for the variety of crafts, toys and other materials, there also needs to be space for adults. A home is not only for learning and growing, but also a place where spending time together as a family is key. So, as a parent, where do you put all of this stuff without it taking over the entire home? Creating a simple, organized and mess-free play space is a large task, but with some pre-planning, it is possible.

Finding that "right" space where there isn't a lot of foot traffic is extremely important. Spend two days observing the common areas of your home. While doing this, make some mental notes as to what areas aren't used often and where adults tend to gather. If there's a corner or a wall of a common room that isn't needed on a regular basis, that's the perfect spot for a play area. When a child is playing, she/he is tapping into their creativity and telling a story. Waiting until the child finishes their play allows that child to complete their story they were creating, whether it's with a baby doll, building blocks, cars and trains - or another favorite toy. Completing tasks without constant interruptions will allow a child to form a beginning, middle and end (a full-circle) of play.

Next, what you should place in this learning environment is dependent on the child's age and developmental level. A toddler will play with something different then a five year old. No matter what age the child is, there are certain "must haves" for their space. These include: a quiet spot (either a bean bag or large pillow), books, puzzles, stuffed animals or baby dolls, an assortment of blocks, art materials and plastic or wood animals. When there are multiple-aged children in your home, be sure to give each one their own space, either by separating their areas - or using two different types of shelving units to visually demonstrate what is theirs.

Organizing materials into functional and workable environments will support the process of learning in a practical, step-by-step fashion. This ensures that the space is easily kept clean and visually pleasing. Each toy should have it's own dedicated space. For small objects, sort them by category and place them in small baskets or plastic bins (balls, cars and trucks, train tracks, books, paper, crayons, etc). If possible, take a picture of the items when they're separated and attach the pictures to their appropriate bin or basket. These containers can be placed on the floor or in a shelving unit against the wall. Provide a children's table, or allow them to take artwork to the main table in your home.

Sometimes children have too many different toys, which can cause toy chaos. Pick out no more than ten to twelve toys, which fall into the categories listed in the above paragraph. Place the rest of the items into large plastic storage bins and put them in a closet, garage or outdoor shed. Children will get bored when they play with the same toys over and over again. A typical toy rotation schedule is every three to four weeks, although some children get tired of toys quicker than others. If you notice the child becomes less engaged with the materials that are set out, rotate them with some of the materials that you put into storage bins. Watch as the child rediscovers their love for a toy they had previously lost interest in.

Lastly, learning to put away toys and stay organized at an early age helps prevent clutter over time - and will also teach children respect for their items. To make sure that the child takes ownership and pride in keeping the play area clean from the start, insist that they every time they are finished with a project or an activity in their play area, they clean up before they transition to another part of the home. Remember to always praise them with "Thank you for listening" or "Wow, you did that all by yourself" when they finish.

If clean up time is a struggle, encourage them to clean up by trying these ideas:

- **Play a clean-up game:** Using your watch, have a race against the clock! How long will it take them to put the toys away?

- **Sing a Song:** The Barney "Clean- Up" Song is a very popular choice.

- **Use this time as a Teachable Moment:** "Let's put all of the red things away first! Can you find all the red items?"

- **Help Out:** Having some help from a parent tends to be a motivator. Example: "You put the trucks away and I will put the balls away".

Pre-K YOUR Way

Level 2 Unit 1

Exploring My Community

Unit 1: Exploring My Community

Themed Items For Indoor Learning Environment

Now that you have set up your environment, you are ready to place materials in it that directly relate to the theme you are studying! Here are some suggestions of materials your child can free-play with during the "Exploring My Community" Theme:

Books: Age-appropriate books that directly correlate with the monthly theme can be found at your local library or bought separately online. This is a great opportunity to take a trip with your child to your local library and go on a search together. Have them identify words or pictures on the cover of children's books that correlate to the theme. Place a variety of books related to the theme in your child's book area. This will increase opportunities for them to expand their knowledge and use what they learn in the activities to comprehend what they read in the books.

Art Area: Encourage your child use this throughout each day by rotating items in an art area. These can be items have already been painted on, paper that they drew on already or leftover materials from another project. Thought provoking art projects are created when children are given unlimited opportunities to explore a variety of materials.

Some suggestions for the art area include:
- Crayons
- Paper
- Pens
- Empty Boxes (all kinds)
- Empty Toilet Paper or Paper Towel Rolls
- Foil
- Clean Q-tips for painting
- Scraps of paper
- Scraps of Yarn
- Scraps of any type of material – including fabric, sand paper, etc.
- Paper Bags
- Straws
- Popsicle Sticks
- Anything else that can be reused.

Sensory Bin Suggestions

A sensory bin is a small plastic bucket that is filled with a variety of materials. Sensory bins provide a space to engage in sensory-rich activities that offer opportunities to investigate textures while providing activities for relaxation and self-regulation. Sensory bins encourage language development, small motor development and control, spatial concepts, problem-solving skills and scientific observations. Each month there are suggested sensory bin materials that correlate with the theme of the unit.

Set Up Instructions: In a Plastic Bucket, rotate the following sensory activities throughout the month.

- **Sand Writing Table:**

  Mix 2 cups of sand, 1 ½ cups cold water and 1 cup of cornstarch together. Stir the mixture for five to ten minutes over medium heat until it becomes thick. Pour the thick sand onto a cookie sheet. After it cools, have your child practice writing the Letter of the Week, Number of the Week and drawing the Shape of the Week in the sand.
  Note: You can also use this mixture to build sand castles that will stick together longer.

- **Natural Bin:**

  Outdoors In the Community there are lots of different Natural Textures. Fill your sensory bins with a variety of natural items such as grass, bark, large rocks, sticks and leaves. Encourage your child to use items to investigate the materials (such as magnifying glass, cups for scooping and child-sized tweezers.

Dramatic Play Area

This play area allows children to understand and experience the adult world through imitation and creativity. The dramatic play area provides a safe space for young children to create stories while practicing new vocabulary and practicing social skills. It is also a space where groups of children engage in pretend play which provides opportunities to learn self-help skills, share space and materials, take turns and the use abstract thinking. Each month there is a list of suggested materials to integrate into this area, which correlate with the theme of the month.

Suggested props to include in the dramatic play/pretend play area include:

- Toy Police Cars, Fire trucks
- Envelopes
- Stamps
- Pretend Money
- Sale Papers
- A Cardboard Box (to pretend as a car)
- Red, Blue and Yellow Paper
- Flashlights
- Maps of your Town

Learning Objectives - Level 2

These activities have been developed to meet specific, age-appropriate, Kindergarten-Readiness skills. These skills are laid out in the learning objectives of each activity. The following activities may be completed in any order desired and are specifically designed to address the academic domains: math, science, language, literacy, cognitive, problem solving, and physical development. **After completing all modules in the Level 2 Curriculum Series, the child should be able to:**

Mathematics

- Identify objects by classification.
- Sort objects into categories by at least one attribute.
- Show understanding of measurement and begin to associate measurement descriptions (big, small, long, short).
- Recite numbers 1 through 10 in order.
- Count objects with one to one correspondence.
- Describe the similarities and differences of several shapes that include circle, triangle, square and rectangle.
- Create and finish simple patterns that include two elements.

Science/ Problem Solving Skills

- Develops solutions to a problem.
- Asks questions and performs simple investigations.
- Works through tasks that are difficult.
- Demonstrates understanding of visual and verbal prompts.

Language and Literacy

- Demonstrate the understanding that letters make words.
- Uses language to talk about past events.
- Uses words and increasing vocabulary to retell a story.
- Uses a variety of vocabulary to describe finding solutions to problems.
- Uses language in conversation to discover answers to questions.
- Name and match Uppercase letters.
- Accurately write all Letters of the Alphabet.
- Demonstrate Phonological Awareness of every Letter (The sounds that letters make).
- Follow simple two-step directions.

Gross Motor/Fine Motor Development

- Uses gross motor movement skills to access a variety of obstacles and environments.
- Hops on one foot, without support, three or more times.
- Runs and Jumps over small objects.
- Uses scissors appropriately.
- Uses a crayon or pencil to draw or write.

Part 1: Exploring My Community Kindergarten Readiness Themed Activities

These activities have been developed to meet specific, age-appropriate, Kindergarten-Readiness skills. These skills are specified in the learning objectives of each activity. The following activities may be completed in any order desired and are specifically designed to address the academic domains: math, science, language, literacy, cognitive, problem solving, and physical development.

Each activity is on its own page. If the adult chooses to print the activities, the space below each activity is provided for adults to write notes regarding the activity. Adults are encouraged to note if the child enjoyed the activity and if the child needs to work on specific learning objectives. Each activity can be repeated more than once to enable the child to master the learning objectives designed for that activity.

A. Math/Science Development

1. Community Count
2. Grocery Store Coupon Hunt
3. A Stamp's Worth
4. Fire and Smoke Detectors
5. Outside Color March

B. Language/Literacy Development

1. Where have I been?
2. Neighbor Names
3. Ways to see my Town
4. City Spots Matching Game
5. My Favorite Place to Go

C. Physical Development- Gross Motor & Fine-Motor

1. Postman Walk
2. Grocery Games
3. Build My City
4. Hello World
5. Fire Hydrant Hunt

Take it to the Next Level: There are some activities which have a component included on how to "take an activity to the next level", increasing skill level related to the learning objectives laid out in that specific activity. Once the child has successful completed an activity, adults are encouraged to try the "take it to the next level" suggestions.

Mathematical Development – Understanding Numbers and their Purpose

By Completing Level 2 Activities, We will learn how to...

- o Identify objects by classification.
- o Sort objects into categories by at least one attribute.
- o Show understanding of measurement and begin to associate measurement descriptions (big, small, long, short).
- o Recite numbers 1 through 10 in order.
- o Count objects with one to one correspondence.
- o Describe the similarities and differences of several shapes that include circle, triangle, square and rectangle.
- o Create and finish simple patterns that include two elements.

Science/Cognitive Development – Learning How to Solve Problems

By Completing Level 2 Activities, We will learn how to..

- o Develop solutions to a problem.
- o Ask questions and performs simple investigations.
- o Work through tasks that are difficult.
- o Demonstrate understanding of visual and verbal prompts

✐ A1. Community Count - Activity time: 20 Minutes

Materials Needed:

☐ One (1) Package of Popsicle Sticks (At least 25 to 40)
☐ One (1) Box of Markers
☐ One (1) Piece of White Paper
☐ One (1) Black Pen

Instructions:

Step 1: Tell your child that together you will find out how many community areas there are in your town.

Step 2: The adult should use a black pen to write the following list of words on a piece of paper:
- Post Office
- Garbage Company
- Grocery Store
- Library
- Fire Station
- Police Station
- Bank

Step 3: Over the course of the week, when you're traveling around town, tell your child to look for each building on the list and make a tally "1" next to each building name.

Example:

Post Office	1 1
Garbage	1
Grocery Store	1 1 1
Library	1
Fire Station	1 1
Police Station	1
Bank	1 1 1 1

Step 4: After one week, ask your child to trace each word (written on the building list from Step 2) using a different color marker for each word. (For example: green marker for Post Office; blue marker for Garbage Company; red marker for Grocery Store, etc.)

Step 5: Ask your child to count the total number of tally marks next to each building name.

Step 6: Ask your child to count out the number of popsicle sticks to match each number of stores they found (from Step 5), placing each popsicle stick group next to the corresponding building name (For Example: 1 popsicle stick for 1 Post office tally; 3 Popsicle Sticks for 3 Grocery Store tallies, etc).

Step 7: Tell your child to color each group of popsicle sticks the same color they traced the word with from step 4 (For example: The child traced the word "post office" with a blue marker. There are five tallies next to the post office. The child should color five popsicle sticks blue.)

Step 8: Tell your child to place each popsicle stick next to the corresponding building word traced with the same color as the popsicle stick. Does the amount of popsicle sticks match the tally mark total in each building category?

Take it to the Next Level:

Allow your child to place the popsicle sticks in their dramatic play area so they can "build" their city. Encourage them to place each popsicle stick around a block structure, that represents the true location of each community building in your city.

A.1 Learning Objectives

Math/Science	Language	Problem Solving	Motor Skills
• Number Sense • One to One Correspondence	• Word Identification • Following New Directions	• Investigating • Categorizing • Matching	• Tracing Letters • Using a Pen

Notes: What did your child do well? Are there any skills they need to continue to work on?

A2. Grocery Store Coupon Hunt - Activity time: 15 minutes

Materials Needed:

- ☐ One (1) Pair of child sized scissors
- ☐ Two (2) Grocery Store Sale Ad Papers
- ☐ One (1) Crayon (any color)

Instructions:

Step 1: Tell your child you're going to plan a shopping trip together to get the food you need for the week. Hand your child the grocery store ads.

Step 2: Allow your child to use the child-safe scissors to cut pictures of foods they would like to purchase at the grocery store. Make sure they cut out the cost of each item as well.

Step 3: Once your child is done, tell them that together, you're going to organize the coupons by how expensive each product is.

Step 4: Using a crayon, ask your child to find and circle the numbers (price) of each item they cut out.

Step 5: Ask your child to sort the coupons by placing all of the items that start with 1 in one pile, all of the items that start with 2 in another pile, all of the items that start with 3 in another pile and so on.

Step 6: Tell your child you have 10 dollars to spend on groceries this trip.

Step 7: Tell the child that we will need to add up the items that they picked to see if it costs more or less than 10 dollars.

Step 8: Help your child add up the **dollar** amount in their ads they cut out. Is the total more or less than 10? If it is more, ask your child what they would take out of the list to make the total cost less than $10.

A.2 Learning Objectives

Math/Science	Language	Problem Solving	Motor Skills
• Number Sense • Classification • Number Identification • Simple Addition and Subtraction • Beginning Budgeting	• Vocabulary Building • Following New Directions	• Develop Solutions • Organization	• Use Scissors Appropriately

Notes: What did your child do well? Are there any skills they need to continue to work on?

✏️ **A3. A Stamp Count** - Activity time: 20 minutes

Materials Needed:

☐ 49 pennies (Or however many pennies it costs for one stamp)
☐ One (1) Postage Stamp
☐ One (1) Box of Crayons
☐ One (1) Black Pen
☐ One (1) Yellow Highlighter
☐ One (1) White Piece of Paper

** **Note:** This activity was created when one stamp was worth 49 cents. If the cost of a stamp has changed, use the current cost for the following activity.

Instructions:

Step 1: Tell your child that when you mail a letter, **one** stamp needs to be placed on the envelope. This is the way you pay the mailman to deliver the mail.

Step 2: Tell your child that each stamp represents an amount of money. Today it costs **49 cents** to mail a letter. When an adult buys a stamp, an adult must pay **49 cents** for that stamp.

Step 3: Show your child the stamp. Allow them to touch it and look at it.

Step 4: Tell your child that this stamp is worth was **49 cents**. We're going to find out how many pennies equal **49.**

Step 5: Place all **49 pennies** on the table.

Step 6: Ask your child to use their pointer finger to move each penny towards them while they count each penny (1 penny, 2 pennies, 3 pennies, etc) all the way until they count all forty-nine pennies. Forty-nine pennies are a lot of pennies!

Step 7: The adult should use the yellow highlighter to write the **number "49"** on the white piece of paper.

Step 8: Encourage your child to trace the number **"49"** with a black pen.

Step 9: Have child use crayons to draw a picture of what they would want their own stamp to look like. Make sure they write the **number "49"** on it.

A.3 Learning Objectives

Math/Science	Language/Literacy	Problem Solving	Motor Skills
• Classification • One to One Correspondence • Numerical Identification	• Use Language in Conversations • Following Two-Step Directions	• Develop solutions • Visual Representation	• Beginning Writing

Notes: What did your child do well? Are there any skills they need to continue to work on?

✏ A4. Smoke Detectors - Activity time: 20 minutes

Materials Needed:

☐ One (1) Piece of plain paper
☐ One (1) Pen
☐ One (1) Yellow highlighter

Instructions:

Step 1: Tell your child that smoke detectors are very important. It is the law to have them in many areas of your home. When there is a fire, the smoke detector will smell the smoke and the alarm will sound. When you hear the sound, everyone needs to get out of the house safely.

Step 2: The adult should fold a blank piece of paper in half.

Step 3: On one half of the paper the adult should write the following list of words:

Bedroom	
Bathroom	
Living Room	
Hallway	
Garage	

Step 4: Tell your child that you're going to walk through the house and find out how many smoke detectors are in each area of your home.

Step 5: The adult should make one tally mark on the paper from Step 3 next to the word describing the type of room the child finds each smoke detector.

Example:

Bedroom	1 1
Bathroom	1
Living Room	1
Hallway	1 1
Garage	1

Step 6: After you have walked through the home, have your child count the total number of tally marks next to each room on the list from Step 5.

Step 7: The adult should use a yellow highlighter to write the numeral representing the total amount of tallies next to each room on the paper from Step 6.

Example:

Bedroom	1 1 2
Bathroom	1 1
Living Room	1 1
Hallway	1 1 2
Garage	1 1

Step 8: Have your child trace the numerals with the pen.

A.4 Learning Objectives

Math/Science	Language/Literacy	Problem Solving	Motor Skills
• Quantity and Counting • One to One Correspondence • Numerical Identification • Classification	• Letter Identification • Understanding Verbal Concepts (Finding Hidden Items)	• Identifying Characteristics • Investigation	• Using a crayon or pencil to draw or write

Notes: What did your child do well? Are there any skills they need to continue to work on?

✎ A5. Outside Color March - Activity time: 20 minutes

Materials Needed:

☐ One (1) Piece of Blank Paper
☐ One (1) Box of Crayons
☐ One (1) Pen
☐ One (1) Yellow Highlighter

Instructions:

Step 1: Tell your child you're going to walk down your street. The adult can decide how long of a walk to take. If your street isn't safe to walk around, then choose a local park, neighborhood or walking trail nearby.

Step 2: Take a box of crayons and a blank piece of paper with you on your walk.

Step 3: Tell your child to use a crayon to make a tally mark for every COL R they see on the walk. When your child sees a color on your walk, they need to use the **same** color crayon to make the tally mark on the piece of paper.

For example:
* Your child found a   flower.

* Ask them to find   crayon to make one tally mark on the sheet of paper.

Step 4: While on your walk, encourage your child to stop and look at a variety of colors (i.e. cars, sticks, houses, trees, fruit, birds, cats, dogs, etc).

Step 5: Once you're done with your walk, return home.

Step 6: Help your child add up the total amount of tally marks by color. Use a highlighter to write the numeral that represents each number.

For Example:

YELLOW FLOWER	1
GREEN GRASS	1
GREEN BUSH	1
GREEN CAR.	1
Total:	4

Step 7: Have your child trace all of the numbers with a pen.

Step 8: Ask your child if they can remember what items they saw on the walk that correspond to each color.

For example:

Adult: "Can you tell me what things you saw on the walk today that were green?"

Child: "I saw a green tree, green grass and a green frog!"

GREEN TREE	1
GREEN GRASS	1
GREEN FROG	1

A.5 Learning Objectives

Math/Science	Language/Literacy	Problem Solving	Motor Skills
• One to One Correspondence • Numerical Identification • Classification	• Use language to talk about past events	• Color Identification • Investigation	• Using a crayon or pencil to draw or write • Tracing

Notes: What did your child do well? Are there any skills they need to continue to work on?

Language Development – Growing our Vocabulary

By Completing Level 2 Activities, We will learn how to...

- Use language to talk about past events.
- Use words and increasing vocabulary to retell a story.
- Use a variety of vocabulary to describe finding solutions to problems.
- Use language in conversation to discover answers to questions.
- Follow simple two-step directions.

Literacy Development – Beginning Reading and Writing

By Completing Level 2 Activities, We will learn how to..

- Demonstrate the understanding that letters make words.
- Name and match Uppercase letters.
- Accurately write all Letters of the Alphabet.
- Demonstrate Phonological Awareness of every Letter (The sounds that letters make).

✎ **B1. Where Have I been?** – This activity spans over two days.

Materials Needed:

☐ One (1) Camera (Adult to use)
☐ Three (3) Blank Pieces of Paper
☐ One (1) Black or Blue Pen
☐ One (1) Yellow Highlighter

Instructions:

Day 1:

Step 1: On the first day, tell the child you're going to take a picture of every place you go.

Step 2: While you're out in your community, the adult should take a picture of all the buildings you visit.

> **For example:** The adult can take a picture of a family or friends house, stores, schools, banks, Post Office and other buildings.

Step 3: That evening, sit down with your child and look at the pictures of the places you visited that day. Ask your child if they can name each place.

Day 2:

The Next Morning:

Step 4: The next morning, tell your child you're going to talk about where you went **yesterday** and where you're going to go **today**.

Step 5: Tell your child you're about to leave and it's their job to remember what places you're visiting today so you can talk about them later tonight. **This time, no one will take any pictures.**

Step 6: While you're out in the community, ask your child if they know the name of the places they see.

In the Evening:

Step 7: That evening, sit down with your child and tell them you're going to compare what you did yesterday to what you did today. This is called **"compare and contrast"**.

Step 8: The adult should write the word **"Yesterday"** on the top on one blank piece of paper.

Step 9: Look through the pictures of where you went yesterday with your child. Use a yellow highlighter to write the names of all the places they see.

Step 10: The adult should write the word **"Today"** on the top of a new blank piece of paper.

Step 11: Ask the child to close their eyes and think about the places they went to that day.

Step 12: Ask the child to tell the adult the names of all the places they went today. Use a yellow highlighter to write down the places the child says. If the child is having a hard time remembering, the adult can give the child clues such as:

- o "We went somewhere where we got food."
- o "We went somewhere where we saw _____."
- o "We went somewhere where I mailed a letter."

Step 13: Ask your child to use a pencil to trace the words written on the pieces of paper titled **"Yesterday"** and **"Today"**.

Step 14: Ask your child if they see any "place" words that are the **same o**n both pieces of paper. Tell them to use a crayon or pen to circle the words that are the **same.** Help your child say the words that are the **same** by sounding out each letter.

Step 15: The adult should write the word **"Tomorrow"** on the top of a new blank piece of paper.

Step 16: Ask your child what places they want to go to **tomorrow**. Use a yellow highlighter to write the names of those places on the piece of paper from Step 14.

Step 17: Ask your child to use a pencil to trace the words written on the paper that says **"Tomorrow"**.

Step 18: Ask your child if they see words that are the same on all three pieces of paper.

Step 19: Tell your child to use a new crayon color to circle the words that are the **same** on all three pieces of paper. Help your child say the words that are the same.

B.1 Learning Objectives

Math/Science	Language/Literacy	Problem Solving	Motor Skills
•Investigating Time (Yesterday, Today and Tomorrow)	•Understanding letters and their purpose •Vocabulary building • Describe past events • Uses language in Conversation •Letter Identification •Beginning Word Identification •Demonstrate knowledge that letters make words	•Picture and Visual Identification • Demonstrates Understanding of Visual and Verbal Prompts • Matching • Understanding Similarities and Differences in Literacy	•Using a crayon or pencil to draw or write •Tracing

Notes: What did your child do well? Are there any skills they need to continue to work on?

✏️ B2. Neighbor Names - Activity time: 30 minutes

Materials Needed:

☐ One (1) Blank Piece of White Paper
☐ One (1) Pen
☐ One (1) Box of Crayons

Instructions:

Step 1: Tell your child you're going to write down the names of your closest neighbors (at least 6). The adult should write the names down on a blank piece of paper using a yellow highlighter.

> ****Note:** If you are unable to write the names of neighbors, write down the name of six family
> members or friends **.

Step 2: Have your child use a pen to trace the names written in Yellow Highlighter.

Step 3: Ask your child to identify all of the letters in each name. Help them sound out the names while they say each letter.

Step 4: Help your child write down their full name (first and last) on the bottom of the same piece of paper.

Step 5: Using one crayon color, have your child circle the **first** letter in their name. Help them name that letter.

Step 6: Ask them to find the same letter (the first letter in their name) in the rest of the names written on the paper. When they see that letter, have them circle the letter using the **same** color crayon they used in step 5.

Step 7: Ask your child to say all of the names that have that letter in it (all of the names that have a letter circled).

Step 8: Using a **new crayon color**, have your child circle the **second** letter in their name. Help them name that letter.

Step 9: Using the **same** crayon color the child used in Step 8, have your child look for the letter they identified (the second letter in their name) in the "neighbor or family/friend" names. When they see that letter, have them circle the letter using the crayon color they used in **step 8.**

Step 10: Ask your child if they can identify all of the names that have the same letter as their **second** letter (all of the names/words that have a letter circled with the crayon color from Step 8).

Step 11: Repeat Steps 8 through 10 until your child has completed all of the letters in their first and last name.

B.2 Learning Objectives

Math/Science	Language/Language	Problem Solving	Motor Skills
•Recognize Numerals	• Letter Identification •Describe similarities and differences of Letter Shapes •Demonstrate knowledge that letters make words	•Memory and Knowledge • Name Identification	•Using a crayon or pencil to draw or write.

Notes: What did your child do well? Are there any skills they need to continue to work on?

Materials Needed:

☐ Four (4) sheets of blank white Paper
☐ One (1) Black Marker
☐ One (1) Yellow Highlighter
☐ One (1) Box of Crayons

Instructions:

Step 1: Ask your child to tell you four different ways to travel around your town (i.e. walk, car, bike, truck, van, run, hike, etc).

Step 2: Using four sheets of blank, white paper, write one word they said in Step 1 on the top of each piece of paper (see example in Step 4 below)

Step 3: Have your child draw a picture representing the word on each piece of paper (see example in Step 4 below).

Step 4: Next, tell the child you're going to change the word into an "action" word. For each picture, write the action word underneath the picture.

Example: If you use a car to get around town, the child would draw a picture of a car on the piece of paper. The adult would then say, "When you're in a car, then you would be 'riding' or 'driving'." The adult would write the word "driving" underneath the picture of the car.

Example:

Step 5: Ask your child if they can find the letters that make all of the nouns into action words ("ing" at the end of each word, turns the word into an action word).

Step 6: Have your child trace the letters "ing" on each action word.

B.3 Learning Objectives

Math/Science	Language/Literacy	Problem Solving	Motor Skills
• Counting 1-4	• Transforming Nouns to Actions • Uses language to talk about a topic • Shows Understanding of Words and their Meaning • Demonstrate knowledge that letters make words	• Demonstrates Visual Representations • Letter Identification	• Using a crayon or pencil to draw or write.

Notes: What did your child do well? Are there any skills they need to continue to work on?

B4. City Spots Match (Complete Activity B1 before completing this activity)
- Activity time: 20 minutes

Materials Needed:

☐ One (1) Stack of Sale Papers (Office Supplies, Garden department, Pet store and Grocery Ads)
☐ One (1) Pair of Child Safe scissors
☐ Five (5) Pieces of blank paper
☐ One (1) Pen
☐ One (1) Glue Stick

Instructions:

Step 1: Tell your child they're going to use pictures to represent different buildings in their community.

Step 2: The adult should use a pen to write the following words on the top of the five pieces of blank paper. There should be **one word** written on each piece of paper:

1. Bank
2. Fire Station
3. Grocery Store
4. Post Office
5. Pet Store

Step 3: Ask your child to use the child safe scissors to cut pictures out of the sale papers that correspond with each place that is written on the papers.

> **Example: Grocery Store**
> Cut our Pictures of: Food, Basket, Cashier, Grocery Bags

Step 4: Have your child glue the pictures on the corresponding piece of paper:

1. **Grocery Store Cut outs** glued on the piece of paper with the word **Grocery Store** written on it.
2. **Bank Cut outs** glued on the piece of paper with the word **Bank** written on it.
3. **Fire Station Cut outs** glued on the piece of paper with the word **Fire Station** written on it.
4. **Post Office Cut outs** glued on the piece of paper with the word **Post Office** written on it.
5. **Pet Store Cut outs** glued on the piece of paper with the word **Pet Store** written on it.

Step 5: Ask your child to count how many pictures they put on each piece of paper. Ask your child why each picture represents that place.

Take it to the Next Level:

Using the places from Activity B1, ask your child if they would like to find some pictures that correspond to the places you visited. Repeat step 3 through 5 using the places from Activity B1.

B.4 Learning Objectives

Math/Science	Language/Literacy	Problem Solving	Motor Skills
• One to One Correspondence	• Word Identification • Using Language to Explain Processes and Reasons	• Memory and Knowledge • Visual Represntation	• Using a crayon or pencil to draw or write. • Using Scissors

Notes: What did your child do well? Are there any skills they need to continue to work on?

✎ **B5. My Favorite Place to Go** - Activity time: 20 minutes

Materials Needed:

☐ Two (2) Pieces of Paper
☐ One (1) Pen
☐ One (1) Box of Crayons

Instructions:

Step 1: Tell your child that together you're going to write a story about their **favorite place to go.**

Step 2: Ask them where their favorite place is. If they have a hard time thinking of a place, ask them if they have a favorite park or walking trail they like to visit.

Step 3: The adult should use a pen and write down what your child said on one of the of blank pieces paper.

Step 4: Ask your child if they can tell you a story about their favorite place. This could be a true story of something that happened there or a reason why they like that place the best. Write down what your child says on the paper from Step 3.

Step 5: Ask your child to describe their favorite place to you. What things are at that place? What do people do there? Write down what they say underneath what you wrote from Step 4.

Where is your favorite place to go?

Tell me a story about this place...

What does this place look like?

What things are at this place?

Step 6: Ask your child to use crayons to draw a picture of their favorite place on a piece of blank paper.

Step 7: Once your child is done, have your child describe everything that is on the picture. The adult should use a pen to label everything your child describes.

Step 8: Re-read the answers/story to your child.

Step 9: Revisit the story throughout the week.

B.5 Learning Objectives

Math/Science	Language/Literacy	Problem Solving	Motor Skills
• None	• Uses a variety of vocabulary • Answers simple questions • Develop the beginning of a story;	• Understands words and Symbols • Recalls significant details	• Using a crayon or pencil to draw or write.

Notes: What did your child do well? Are there any skills they need to continue to work on?

Gross Motor – Using our large muscles to move!

By Completing Level 2 Activities, We will learn...

- Uses gross motor movement skills to access a variety of obstacles and environments.
- Hops on one foot, without support, three or more times.
- Runs and Jumps over small objects.

Fine Motor – Using our hands to complete tasks

By Completing Level 2 Activities, We will learn...

- Uses scissors appropriately.
- Uses a crayon or pencil to draw or write.

✎ C1. Postman Walk - Activity time: 30 minutes

Materials Needed:

☐ Ten (10) 3x5 Index Cards
☐ One (1) Black Marker
☐ One (1) Street with Mailboxes or House numbers

Instructions:

Step 1: The adult should use a black marker to write the number **1 through 10** on each of the 3x5 index cards **(Write only ONE number on each card).**

Step 2: Once completed, tell the child that you are going to go on a number hunt.

Step 4: Together, walk around the neighborhood with your child. Every time you see a mailbox, or house number, have your child look through the 3x5 index cards and match the numbers to the mailbox numbers.

Step 5: Tell your child the name of each number. Encourage them to repeat the name of the number.

C.1 Learning Objectives

Math/Science	Language/Literacy	Problem Solving	Motor Skills
• Number Sense: Quantity and Counting • Discovering Numbers • Identifying Numerals	• Learning Names of Numbers	• Matching	• Walking

Notes: What did your child do well? Are there any skills they need to continue to work on?

Materials Needed:

☐ One (1) Green Piece of Construction Paper
☐ One (1) Blue Piece of Construction Paper
☐ One (1) White Piece of Construction Paper
☐ One (1) Yellow Piece of Construction Paper
☐ One (1) Red Piece of Construction Paper
☐ One (1) Brown Piece of Construction Paper
☐ One (1) Pair of Child Safe Scissors
☐ One (1) Glue Stick
☐ One (1) Roll of Painter's Tape
☐ One (1) Grocery Store Sale papers

Instructions:

Step 1: The adult should place the pieces of construction paper in a line.

Step 2: Tell the child to look through the grocery store ads and use child-safe scissors to cut out pictures of items that match the colors of the construction paper (food items that are blue, green, red, yellow, white, brown and red).

Step 3: Tell the child to sort the pieces from Step 2 by placing the pieces on the construction paper that is the same color (example: green foods on the green construction paper).

Step 4: Once the sorting is complete, have the child glue each piece of food onto the corresponding construction paper.

Step 5: Once completed, the adult should use painter's tape to tape each piece of colored paper to the floor. They can be taped in a pattern, a circle or a line.

Step 6: Tell the child to **hop** to the construction paper that is the color that the adult says. The adult should shout out the following color patterns (Repeat the patterns at least four times):

1. Green, **Blue**, Green, **Blue**, Green, **Blue**

2. Red,   , Red,   , Red,

3. White, Green, **Blue**, White, Green, **Blue**, White, Green, **Blue**

4. Red, White,   , Red, White,   , Red, White,   ,

Take it to the Next Level:

Can your child come up with more color patterns to hop to? If not, the adult can help them mix the colors up to make more "hopping" patterns of 3 to 4 colors.

C.2 Learning Objectives

Math/Science	Language/Literacy	Problem Solving	Motor Skills
• Categorizing	• Following Directions	• Color Identification • Create Simple Patterns	• Gross Motor: Hopping • Fine Motor: Using Scissors Appropriately • Fine Motor: Using a Glue Stick

Notes: What did your child do well? Are there any skills they need to continue to work on?

✎ **C3. Build My City -** Activity time: 20 – 40 minutes

Materials Needed:

☐ Unlimited amount of the following:
  ○ Empty tissue boxes
  ○ Empty toilet paper rolls
  ○ Empty paper towel rolls
  ○ Tape (Optional)
  ○ Blocks of any kind
  ○ Empty Cardboard Boxes
  ○ Cardboard pieces

Instructions:

Step 1: Tell the child you're going to **build** the city you live in.

Step 2: Find a level, open, indoor or outdoor space.

Step 3: Tell the child they are going to follow simple directions to build their city together.

Step 4: The adult should place all of the items from the materials list on the floor, at least 10 feet away from the "**building site**" in Step 1.

Step 5: Group all similar materials together (example: all of the empty toilet paper rolls together, all of the empty paper towel rolls together, etc).

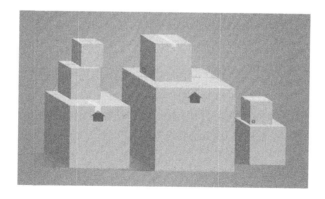

Step 6: Ask your child what building they would like to build first (example: mall, shopping center, fire station, post office, bank, school, etc).

Step 7: Tell your child they need to listen to your directions **before** they retrieve an object.

Step 8: Tell your child the following **Game Rule:** They can only move **ONE** object at a time

Step 9: Ask your child which object they would like to use **first** to build their building. Ask them to pick that item up from the floor.

Step 10: Look at the list below to find out what **ACTION** the child needs to do when moving the **object** (from step 9) to their **building "site"** (the flat and level location from Step 2).

For example: If the child wants to use a paper towel roll, the child has to pick up the paper towel roll from the pile of paper towels, then jump to the spot where the building will be built.

Object	Action
Empty Tissue Box	**Roll on the floor holding the tissue box**
Empty toilet paper rolls	Hop on one foot holding the toilet paper roll
Empty paper towel rolls	Jump with two feet holding the paper towel roll
Tape (Optional)	Flap their Arms like a Bird
Blocks of any kind	**Spin in circles while holding the block**
Empty Cardboard Boxes	Crawl like a baby while holding the cardboard box
Cardboard pieces	Balance the cardboard piece on your head

Step 11: Use the following **two-step direction format** using the Object-Association List in Step 10. Repeat until they complete their building.

> **Two-Step Direction Format**: "(Pick up the (**object**) and (**action**) to the (**building**)".

> **Example:** "Pick up the **cardboard piece** and balance the cardboard piece on your head while you walk back to **the building site**".

Step 12: Repeat step 11 until they complete their building.

C.3 Learning Objectives

Math/Science	Language/Literacy	Problem Solving	Motor Skills
•Categorizing	•Following 2-Step Directions	•Memory and Knowledge	•Gross Motor: Balance and Coordination

Notes: What did your child do well? Are there any skills they need to continue to work on?

✏ C4. Hello Round World - Activity time: 20 minutes

Materials Needed:

☐ One (1) Piece of Sidewalk Chalk
☐ One (1) Outdoor Space

Instructions:

Step 1: Tell your child you're going to identify where they live in the world.

Step 2: Using a piece of sidewalk chalk, the adult should draw **four circles.**

1. First draw one large circle with a **diameter of four feet**.
2. Draw a second circle inside the first circle with a **diameter of three feet**.
3. Draw a third circle inside the second circle with a **diameter of two feet.**
4. Draw a fourth circle inside the third circle with a **diameter of one foot.**

   Example:

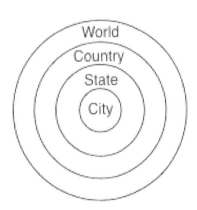

Step 3: Inside the **Largest Circle,** write the word **"World".**

Step 4: Inside the **Second Largest Circle**, write the name of the **Country you live in.**

Step 5: Inside the **Third Largest Circle,** write the name of the **State you live in.**

Step 6: Inside the **Smallest Circle,** write the first Letter of the **City you live in.**

Step 7: Ask your child if they can tell you what shape you drew **(Answer: Circles).**

Step 8: Ask your child: "**Why** is the shape is a circle?" Answer: it is round and has no corners.

Step 9: Explain to your child that everyone lives in the great big world. Inside the world there are countries. Inside the countries there are states. Inside the states there are cities.

Step 10: While pointing to each circle, repeat the following phrases while filling in the blanks:

- "We live in the Country: _____."
- "We live in the State: _____."
- "We live in the City: _____."

Step 11: We're going to play a hopping game! The adult is going to say the name of a place and the child should hop, on one foot, into the circle that was named.

Repeat the following sentences, filling in the blank with the names written in the circle:

- "I live in the big round world." (Child should hop into the largest circle that says "world").
- "I live in the city called _____." (Child should hop into the circle with name of city).
- "I live in the country called _____." (Child should hop the circle with name of country).
- "I live in the state called _____." (Child should hop the circle with name of state).

Step 12: Repeat as long as you would like.

Step 13: Can your child remember which circle is the largest? Which one is the smallest?

C.4 Learning Objectives

Math/Science	Language/Literacy	Problem Solving	Motor Skills
• Understanding Shapes • Investigating the World	• Following Directions • Letter and Word Identification • Vocabulary Building	• Big vs. Little • Comparison	• Gross Motor: Jumping • Gross Motor: Hopping • Gross Motor: Balance and Coordination

Notes: What did your child do well? Are there any skills they need to continue to work on?

✏️ **C5. Where is the closest Fire Hydrant -** Activity time: 20 minutes

Materials Needed:

☐ One (1) House that has a fire hydrant in the neighborhood
☐ One (1) Pen
☐ One (1) Piece of Paper

Instructions:

Step 1: It's time to go on a search to find the closest fire hydrant! Tell your child that fire hydrants are important because if there is a fire in a home, the fireman can use water from the fire hydrant to put out the fire. Walk with your child to the closest fire hydrant.

Step 2: Stand outside, in front of your door.

Step 3: Ask your child to walk to the closest fire hydrant and count how many steps it takes for them to get there. (Make sure to walk with your child.)

Step 4: The adult should use a pen to write down how many steps it took for the child to walk to the fire hydrant.

Step 5: Tell your child to go back to the front of your home.

Step 6: Ask your child to walk to the same fire hydrant, but this time take **LARGE** steps to get there. Count how many large steps it takes to get to the fire hydrant.

Step 7: Once the child reaches the fire hydrant, the adult should use a pen to write down the number **LARGE** of steps it took.

Step 8: Ask your child if the total number of **LARGE** steps is **MORE** or **LESS** than the number of steps it took the first time they walked to the fire hydrant. The adult can help them figure out the answer by comparing the numbers written on the paper.

Step 9: Repeat Steps 6 through 8 using the following **actions**:

   ○ Jumping - Count the total jumps its take to get to the fire hydrant
   ○ Tip-Toeing - Count the total tip-toe steps its take to get to the fire hydrant
   ○ Skipping - Count the total skips its take to get to the fire hydrant

Step 10: When you are through, ask your child if there is another way they can think of to get to the fire hydrant. Continue comparing steps.

C.5 Learning Objectives

Math/Science	Language/Literacy	Problem Solving	Motor Skills
•Counting •One to One Correspondence •Numeral Identification	•Following Directions	•More vs. Less •Compare and Contrast	•Gross Motor: Walking different Steps •Gross Motor: Jumping •Gross Motor: Tip-Toe Walking •Gross Motor: Skipping •Gross Motor: Balance and Coordination

Notes: What did your child do well? Are there any skills they need to continue to work on?

Pre-K YOUR Way
Level 2 Unit 2

Roadways and Signs

Unit 2: Roadways and Signs

Themed Items For Indoor Learning Environment

Now that you have set up your environment, you are ready to place materials in it that directly relate to the theme you are studying! Here are some suggestions of materials your child can free-play with during the "Roadways and Signs Theme:

Books: Age-appropriate books that directly correlate with the monthly theme can be found at your local library or bought separately online. This is a great opportunity to take a trip with your child to your local library and go on a search together. Have them identify words or pictures on the cover of children's books that correlate to the theme. Place a variety of books related to the theme in your child's book area. This will increase opportunities for them to expand their knowledge and use what they learn in the activities to comprehend what they read in the books.

Art Area: Encourage your child use this throughout each day by rotating items in an art area. These can be items have already been painted on, paper that they drew on already or leftover materials from another project. Thought provoking art projects are created when children are given unlimited opportunities to explore a variety of materials.

Some suggestions for the art area include:
- Crayons
- Paper
- Pens
- Empty Boxes (all kinds)
- Empty Toilet Paper or Paper Towel Rolls
- Foil
- Clean Q-tips for painting
- Scraps of paper
- Scraps of Yarn
- Scraps of any type of material – including fabric, sand paper, etc.
- Paper Bags
- Straws
- Popsicle Sticks
- Anything else that can be reused.

Sensory Bin Suggestions

A sensory bin is a small plastic bucket that is filled with a variety of materials. Sensory bins provide a space to engage in sensory-rich activities that offer opportunities to investigate textures while providing activities for relaxation and self-regulation. Sensory bins encourage language development, small motor development and control, spatial concepts, problem-solving skills and scientific observations. Each month there are suggested sensory bin materials that correlate with the theme of the unit.

Set Up Instructions: In a Plastic Bucket, rotate the following sensory activities throughout the month.

- **Sand Writing Table:**

  Mix 2 cups of sand, 1 ½ cups cold water and 1 cup of cornstarch together. Stir the mixture for five to ten minutes over medium heat until it becomes thick. Pour the thick sand onto a cookie sheet. After it cools, have the child practice writing the Letter of the Week, writing the number of the week and drawing the Shape of the week on the sand. *Note: You can also use this mixture to build sand castles that will stick together longer.*

- **"Stop and Go" Goo:**

  Roadways are full of different obstacles, such as tunnels, bridges, signs, pedestrians, railroad tracks and more. Place some moldable "Goo" into the child container. To make this "Goo" mix 2 parts flour to 1 part vegetable oil. The child can help mix it together. Add more flour if the "goo" is too runny.

  a. Add some plastic cars, sticks and leaves.
  b. Allow the child to use food coloring to "dye" some of the "Goo" red, green or yellow so they can use that "Goo" to tell cars to stop, go or slow down.
  c. Add in small plastic people or animals
  d. Allow the child to add small empty boxes or toilet paper rolls to make bridges and tunnels.

Dramatic Play Area

This play area allows children to understand and experience the adult world through imitation and creativity. The dramatic play area provides a safe space for young children to create stories while practicing new vocabulary and practicing social skills. It's also a space where groups of children engage in pretend play providing opportunities to learn self-help skills, share space and materials, take turns and the use abstract thinking. Each month there is a list of suggested materials to integrate into this area, which correlates with the theme of the month.

Suggested props to include in the Roadways and Signs dramatic play/pretend play area include:

- A piece of cardboard or long piece of butcher paper for the child to draw roadways on
- Sidewalk chalk to draw roadways outdoors
- Red, Green, Yellow, Blue and White paper
- Pictures of Roadways in different parts of the world
- Car Magazines
- Different sized paper, cut into circles, pentagons and octagons
- Car seat
- Jacket
- Outdoor shoes (rain boots, hiking boots, tennis shoes)
- A steering Wheel cover
- Large Boxes
- Plastic/Fabric tunnel
- Baby dolls
- Plastic cars
- Anything else the child can think she/he may need for their roadways or car?

Learning Objectives - Level 2

These activities have been developed to meet specific, age-appropriate, Kindergarten-Readiness skills. These skills are laid out in the learning objectives of each activity. The following activities may be completed in any order desired and are specifically designed to address the academic domains: math, science, language, literacy, cognitive, problem solving, and physical development. **After completing all modules in the Level 2 Curriculum Series, the child should be able to:**

Mathematics

- Identify objects by classification.
- Sort objects into categories by at least one attribute.
- Show understanding of measurement and begin to associate measurement descriptions (big, small, long, short).
- Recite numbers 1 through 10 in order.
- Count objects with one to one correspondence.
- Describe the similarities and differences of several shapes that include circle, triangle, square and rectangle.
- Create and finish simple patterns that include two elements.

Science/ Problem Solving Skills

- Develops solutions to a problem.
- Asks questions and performs simple investigations.
- Works through tasks that are difficult.
- Demonstrates understanding of visual and verbal prompts.

Language and Literacy

- Demonstrate the understanding that letters make words.
- Uses language to talk about past events.
- Uses words and increasing vocabulary to retell a story.
- Uses a variety of vocabulary to describe finding solutions to problems.
- Uses language in conversation to discover answers to questions.
- Name and match Uppercase letters.
- Accurately write all Letters of the Alphabet.
- Demonstrate Phonological Awareness of every Letter (The sounds that letters make).
- Follow simple two-step directions.

Gross Motor/Fine Motor Development

- Uses gross motor movement skills to access a variety of obstacles and environments.
- Hops on one foot, without support, three or more times.
- Runs and Jumps over small objects.
- Uses scissors appropriately.
- Uses a crayon or pencil to draw or write.

Roadways and Signs Kindergarten Readiness Themed Activities

These activities have been developed to meet specific, age-appropriate, Kindergarten-Readiness skills. These skills are specified in the learning objectives of each activity. The following activities may be completed in any order desired and are specifically designed to address the academic domains: math, science, language, literacy, cognitive, problem solving, and physical development.

Each activity is on its own page. If the adult chooses to print the activities, the space below each activity is provided for adults to write notes regarding the activity. Adults are encouraged to note if the child enjoyed the activity and if the child needs to work on specific learning objectives. Each activity can be repeated more than once to enable the child to master the learning objectives designed for that activity.

A. Math/Science Development

1. Color the Road
2. One Way/Two Ways
3. How Many Lanes
4. Neighborhood Walk
5. Stop Light Pattern

B. Language/Literacy Development

1. STOP! Dead End!
2. License Plate Name
3. Speed Limit Number March
4. Children Crossing
5. My Street Name

C. Physical Development- Gross Motor & Fine-Motor

1. Freeway
2. Curvy Roads
3. Construction Zone
4. Bridges Over _____
5. Through a _____ Tunnel

Take it to the Next Level: There are some activities which have a component included on how to "take an activity to the next level", increasing skill level related to the learning objectives laid out in that specific activity. Once the child has successfully completed an activity, adults are encouraged to try the "take it to the next level" suggestions.

A. Mathematical Development – Understanding Numbers and their Purpose

By Completing Level 2 Activities, We will learn how to…

- o Identify objects by classification.
- o Sort objects into categories by at least one attribute.
- o Show understanding of measurement and begin to associate measurement descriptions (big, small, long, short).
- o Recite numbers 1 through 10 in order.
- o Count objects with one to one correspondence.
- o Describe the similarities and differences of several shapes that include circle, triangle, square and rectangle.
- o Create and finish simple patterns that include two elements.

Science/Cognitive Development – Learning How to Solve Problems

By Completing Level 2 Activities, We will learn how to..

- o Develop solutions to a problem.
- o Ask questions and performs simple investigations.
- o Work through tasks that are difficult.
- o Demonstrate understanding of visual and verbal prompts

A1. Color the Road - Activity time: 30 minutes

Materials Needed:

- ☐ One (1) Piece of Sidewalk Chalk
- ☐ Five (5) Piece of Blue Paper (Any size)
- ☐ Four (4) Pieces of Red Paper (Any size)
- ☐ Three (3) Pieces of Yellow Paper (Any size
- ☐ Two (2) Pieces of Green Paper (Any size)
- ☐ One (1) Piece of White Paper (Any size)

Instructions:

Step 1: Tell your child they're going to create a city with roadways using sidewalk chalk.

Step 2: Encourage your child to use a piece of sidewalk chalk to make **any shape** roadway they would like. It can be a straight line, curvy or circular.

Step 3: Tell them that the edges of a sidewalk are called curbs. Sometimes these curbs have colors painted on them. Each color means something different. The child is going to have an opportunity to place colored paper alongside the "road" they drew to give directions to the drivers.

Step 4: First, show your child the 5 pieces of Blue paper. Tell him/her that if someone is **hurt, injured, or has a disability,** they're able to get a blue sign that allows them to park in front of a blue curb.

Step 5: Ask your child to count how many blue pieces of paper there are (Answer: 5 blue).

Step 6: Ask your child to pick **five spots** alongside the road they drew, where they would like to place blue paper for people with handicap signs.

Step 7: Show your child the 4 pieces of red paper. Tell them that sidewalks with red curbs are spaces for emergency vehicles (like fire trucks or ambulances) to park.

Step 8: Ask them to count how many red pieces of paper there are (Answer: 4 red).

Step 9: Allow your child to place the red paper along **four different spots** of the road for emergency vehicles to park.

Step 10: Show the child the   . Tell them sidewalks that have   on them are for **big trucks or cars to load or unload things.**

Step 11: Ask the child to count how many   of paper there are
Step 12: Allow the child to **pick three spots** to place the   along the road they drew, where   .

Step 13: Show the child two pieces of green paper. Tell them that if they see a curb painted green, that means a car can only park there for a short amount of time. Sometimes it's 10 minutes, 20 minutes, 30 minutes or more.

Step 14: Ask your child to count how many green pieces of paper there are (Answer: 2).

Step 15: Allow your child to place the green papers along the road they drew where the cars should have limited parking time. Ask them how long they want the time limit to be? The adult should write that number on each green piece of paper.

Step 16: Show your child a piece of **white** paper. Tell them that sometimes curbs are painted **white**. These areas are for **cars to pick up or drop people off.**

Step 17: Ask your child to count how **many white pieces** of paper there are **(Answer: 1).**

Step 18: Allow the child to pick **one** spot along the road they drew, **where they would like to designate as a pick-up/drop-off area for people**.

Step 19: Allow your child to use sidewalk chalk to draw buildings and a city around their road and papers.

Step 20: Ask your child what the **colored paper represent**. Can they remember?

Step 21: Encourage your child to use toy cars to drive around the track. **Make sure they stop and follow all curb "directions" when parking.**

Take it to the Next Level:

When you're walking or driving around your community and see painted curbs, ask the child what the color it is and what it represents. Can they remember?

A.1 Learning Objectives

Math/Science	Language	Problem Solving	Motor Skills
• Number Sense • One to One Correspondence	• Following New Directions • Increasing Vocabulary	• Color Identification • Categorizing • Matching • Understanding Symbolic Meaning	• Fine Motor: Using a writing tool (Sidewalk Chalk)

Notes: What did your child do well? Are there any skills they need to continue to work on?

A2. One Way vs. Two Way - Activity time: 15 minutes

Materials Needed:

- ☐ One (1) Green Crayon
- ☐ One (1) Blue Crayon
- ☐ One (1) Piece of Blank White Paper
- ☐ One (1) Yellow Crayon
- ☐ One (1) Pen

Instructions:

Step 1: Tell your child that there are different streets in the city. Some streets have two lanes.

Step 2: Fold the blank piece of paper in half.

Step 3: Ask the child to use the green crayon to draw **two lines**, parallel to each other, across one half of the paper. See example below:

Step 4: Tell the child that each of those lines represents **one lane** on a street.

Step 5: Ask your child to use the pen to draw **one arrow on the same end of each line**. Each arrow should be pointing in the same direction:

These **two lanes** represent a **one-way street**. That means that even though there are two lanes, the cars in each lane must go the same direction.

Step 6: Next, have the child use the green crayon to draw one green line and use the blue crayon to draw a blue line next to it. See following example:

Step 7: Tell the child to draw one arrow at the end of the green line. Then draw one arrow on **opposite side** on the blue line. Each arrow should point into the **opposite directions**:

The green line arrow points in one direction and the blue line arrow points in the opposite direction. That means that one car in the green lane would drive one way and another car in blue lane would drive the other way. **This is a two-way street because the cars can drive in two directions.**

Step 8: Encourage your child to use toy cars to demonstrate a **one-way street**. Ask them to drive two cars, side by side, in the same direction.

** Note: If the child doesn't have toy cars, have them pretend to move a small object, such as a raisin, along the lines.

Step 9: Encourage your child to use the toy cars to demonstrate a **two-way street**. One car drives one direction on the green line and another car drive the other way on the blue line.

Take it to the Next Level:

Allow your child to use sidewalk chalk to draw one-way and two-way roads on the sidewalk. Using their toy cars, encourage them to drive on the. The adult can yell out "one way" or "two way" – see if your child changes the directions of the cars based on the type of road you yell out!

A.2 Learning Objectives

Math/Science	Language	Problem Solving	Motor Skills
• Number Sense • Classification	• Vocabulary Building • Following New Directions	• Develop Solutions • Visual Representation	• Fine Motor: Using writing materials

Notes: What did your child do well? Are there any skills they need to continue to work on?

✎ A3. How Many Lanes - Activity time: 20 minutes

Materials Needed:

☐ Three (3) Popsicle Sticks
☐ One (1) Yellow Marker
☐ One (1) Green Marker
☐ One (1) Orange Marker
☐ One (1) Flat surface
☐ One (1) Black Pen

Instructions:

Step 1: Tell your child you're going to talk about the different lanes on a freeway. There **are three lanes** on your freeway that you're going to make.

Step 2: Tell your child to use   to color **one popsicle stick**

Step 3: Help the child write the **number "1"** on the

Step 4: Tell the child to use the green marker to color one popsicle stick green.

Step 5: Help the child write the **number "2"** on the green popsicle stick.

Step 6: Tell the child to use the orange marker to color one popsicle stick orange.

Step 7: Help the child write the number "3" on the orange popsicle stick.

Step 8: Encourage the child to place the **three popsicle sticks in a line, on a smooth, flat surface**: (Example: tile or wood floor).

The   stick should be placed on the surface **first.** Have them place the orange stick to the **left of the yellow popsicle stick**. Then have the child place the green stick **to the left of the orange popsicle stick.   See example below:**

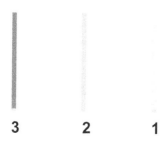

3   2   1

Step 9: Tell the child the popsicle stick with the **number 1 is the right lane.**

Step 10: Tell the child the popsicle stick with the **number 2 is the middle lane.**

Step 11: Tell the child the popsicle stick with the **number 3 is the left lane.**

Step 12: Tell the child they're going to be a **"car"**! They will use their pointer finger to push each "lane" across the floor. **Whichever lane goes the farthest wins!**

Step 13: Have the child put their **pointer finger** on the popsicle stick with the **number 1 on it.**

Step 14: Tell them to push the tip of the popsicle stick so it slides across the floor.

Step 15: Have the child put their **pointer finger** on the popsicle stick with the **number 2 on it.**

Step 16: Tell them to push the tip of the popsicle stick so it slides across the floor.

Step 17: Have the child put their **pointer finger** on the popsicle stick with **the number 3 on it.**

Step 18: Tell them to push the tip of the popsicle stick so it slides across the floor.

Step 19: Ask the child which popsicle stick went the farthest! **What number is it**? **What color is it**?

Step 20: Tell your child that on freeway, the lane on the RIGHT goes the SLOWEST, the lane in the MIDDLE goes the MEDIUM speed and the lane on the LEFT goes the FASTEST!

Step 21: Tell your child to look at the numbers written on the popsicle sticks. Ask them to put them in order, from **left to right**, the left side with the **largest** number (3) and the right side with the **smallest** number (1) .

Step 22: Does your child understand the words: left, middle and right? How about largest, medium and smallest?

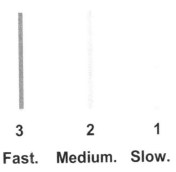

3	2	1
Fast.	**Medium.**	**Slow.**

Step 21: Repeat step 13 through 19 as many times as the child would like.

A.3 Learning Objectives

Math/Science	Language	Problem Solving	Motor Skills
• Number Sense • Classification • One to One Correspondence	• Vocabulary Building • Following New Directions • Understanding New Words • Understanding Opposites	• Numbers as Symbols • Identifying Colors • Visual Representation • Discovering Directions	• Fine Motor: Using writing materials • Fine Motor: Writing numbers • Fine Motor: Isolating Pointer Finger

Notes: What did your child do well? Are there any skills they need to continue to work on?

✎ A4. Neighborhood Walk - Activity time: 20 minutes

Materials Needed:

☐ Two (2) Pieces of Paper
☐ One (1) Pen
☐ One (1) Box of Crayons
☐ A safe neighborhood to walk around

Instructions:

Step 1: Tell your child you're going to go on a sign hunt.

Step 2: The adult should use a pen to write down the following words on one piece of blank paper:

1. Stop
2. Child Crossing
3. Speed Limit
4. Street Name
5. Yield

Step 3: It's time for a walk! Point out each of the signs listed in Step 2 when you see them. If you want, take a photo of your child posing in front of each sign.

Step 4: When the child points out of the signs, the adult should make a tally mark next to that sign on the piece of paper from Step 2.

Step 5: Are there any signs that you see on your walk that is not listed on the list from Step 2? If so, write the names down on the piece of paper.

Step 6: Once you have finished your walk, have your child count up the total number of tallies next to each sign you found. **For example:**

- **Stop Sign 5**
- **Child Crossing 3**
- **Speed Limit Sign 2**

Step 7: Next, the adult should draw a graph on the blank piece of white paper.

See Example below:

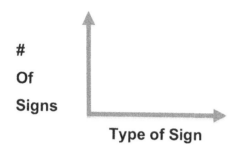

Step 8: The adult should use crayons to highlight each sign on the list from Step 2. Each word should be traced/highlighted with a different color.

For example:

- Stop sign 5
- Child Crossing 3
- Speed Limit Sign 2
- **Street Name Sign 7**
- Yield Sign 1

Step 9: The adult and child should use the graph from Step 7, and the highlighted words from Step 8 to create a category graph. Use the same colors the sign titles are traced with (from Step 8) to draw one box for each type of sign found (total tallies from Step 6).

For Example:

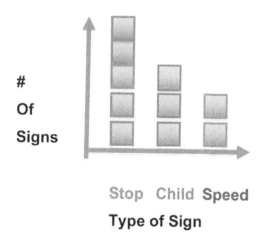

Step 10: Ask the child to count up each box. Does the amount of boxes drawn for each sign match the amount of tallies (in Steps 4 and 5) for each sign they saw?

Step 11: Ask the child which sign they saw more of?

Step 12: Ask the child which sign they saw the least of?

Step 13: Ask the child to count up ALL of the boxes on the graph. How many signs did they see total?

A.4 Learning Objectives

Math/Science	Language	Problem Solving	Motor Skills
•Number Sense •Classification •One to One Correspondence •Beginning Graphing/Charting •Data Collection •Beginning Addition	•Vocabulary Building •Following New Directions •Understanding Size Words	•Identifying Street Signs and their Meanings •Visual Representation •Object Identification	•Fine Motor: Using writing materials •Fine Motor: Writing numbers

Notes: What did your child do well? Are there any skills they need to continue to work on?

A5. Yellow, Red and Green - Activity time: 20 minutes

Materials Needed:

☐ Red Construction Paper
☐ Green Construction Paper
☐ Yellow Construction Paper
☐ One (1) Pair of adult scissors

Instructions:

Step 1: The adult should use scissors to cut out **five** equal sized circles out of the red construction paper.

Step 2: The adult should use scissors to cut out **five** equal sized circles out of the green construction paper.

Step 3: The adult should use scissors to cut out **five** equal sized circles out of the

Step 4: Mix the circles together and place them on a table.

Step 5: Ask your child to sort the circles into **three piles**: green circles, red circles and

Step 6: Tell your child the green circle lights at stoplights mean "Go", the mean   and the red lights mean "Stop".

Step 7: Next, tell the child you're going to make a pattern with the "lights".

Step 8: Tell the child you're going to tell them what circle to pick up by saying what they mean on a stoplight ("go" = green circle; "slow" =   ; "stop" = red circle).

Step 9: Say the following words/pattern and see if the child can pick out the corresponding circle:

- Go, go, stop (answer: green, green, **red**)

Step 10: Ask the child if they can add to the pattern by repeating it:

Step 11: Repeat Step 9 and Step 10 with the following Patterns:

- Go, stop, go, stop   (Answer: green, **red**, green, **red**)

- Slow, go, slow, go   (Answer: yellow, green, yellow, green)

- Go, stop, stop, go, stop, stop (Answer: green, **red**, **red**, green, **red**, **red**)

- Slow, slow, stop, slow, slow, stop (Answer: yellow, yellow, **red**, yellow, yellow, **red**)

Take it to the Next Level: Can the child think of more patterns to try? How about a pattern with three different items such as:

- Slow, stop, go, slow, stop, go (Answer: yellow, red, green, yellow, red, green)
- Slow, Slow, Stop, Go, Go (Answer: yellow, yellow, red, green, green)

A.5 Learning Objectives

Math/Science	Language	Problem Solving	Motor Skills
•Classification •One to One Correspondence •Patterning	•Vocabulary Building •Following New Directions	•Color Identification •Visual Representation •Categorizing/Sorting	•N/A

Notes: What did your child do well? Are there any skills they need to continue to work on?

Language Development – Growing our Vocabulary

By Completing Level 2 Activities, We will learn how to...

- Use language to talk about past events.
- Use words and increasing vocabulary to retell a story.
- Use a variety of vocabulary to describe finding solutions to problems.
- Use language in conversation to discover answers to questions.
- Follow simple two-step directions.

Literacy Development – Beginning Reading and Writing

By Completing Level 2 Activities, We will learn how to..

- Demonstrate the understanding that letters make words.
- Name and match Uppercase letters.
- Accurately write all Letters of the Alphabet.
- Demonstrate Phonological Awareness of every Letter (The sounds that letters make).

B1. STOP Dead End! - Activity time: 15 minutes

Materials Needed:

☐ One (1) Piece of Red Paper
☐ One (1) Pair of Adult Sized Sciss
☐ One (1) Black Marker

Instructions:

Step 1: The adult should use scissors to cut an **Octagon** (the same shape of a stop sign which has **eight sides**) out of the red piece of paper.

Step 2: The adult should use the pen to write the word **"STOP"** inside the stop sign.

Step 3: Tell your child that some roads have a dead end. That means the road ends at a building, an empty space or a body of water.

Step 4: Tell the child it's time to write a story. Tell the child the adult is going to say a sentence. When the adult says **"uh oh"** the child should hold up the sign and say "Stop".

Step 5: The adult will finish the sentence and the **child will fill in the blank** with an **object, place or landscape.** Example:

- **Adult:** **"One day I was walking along the road and passed a school. "uh oh"….**
- **Child:** Hold up the stop sign.
- **Adult:** **"There was a Dead End! If I would have kept walking, I would have walked into a**…
- **Child:** Should finish the sentence (Example: "River").

Step 6: Complete the following phrases with the same directions as in Step 6:

1. "One day I was **driving** to the store and... **"uh oh"** (child hold Stop Sign). "There was a **Dead End**! If I would have kept **driving**, I would have **driven** into a ____(child should fill in the blank)_____!"

2. "One day I was **running** up a hill and... **"uh oh"** (child hold Stop Sign). There was a **Dead End**! If I would have kept **running**, I would have **run** into a ____(child should fill in the blank)_____!"

3. "One day I was **walking** my puppy and... **"uh oh"** (child hold Stop Sign). There was a **Dead End**! If I would have kept **walking**, I would have **walked** into a ____(child should fill in the blank)_____!"

4. "One day I was **driving** to my school and... **"uh oh"** (child hold Stop Sign). There was a **Dead End**! If I would have kept **driving,** I would have **driven** into a ____(child should fill in the blank)_____!"

5. "One day I was **walking** to the Post Office and... **"uh oh"** (child hold Stop Sign). There was a **Dead End**! If I would have kept **walking**, I would have walked into a ____(child should fill in the blank)_____!"

Take it to the Next Level:

Now switch roles. The child can come up with a scenario and the adult should hold up the stop sign. See example below:

- Child: "One day I _____ and **"uh oh"** "
- Adult: Hold up the Stop Sign.
- Child: "There was a **Dead End**! If I would have kept **walking,** I would have walked into a _____
- Adult fill in the blank: _____!

B.1 Learning Objectives

Math/Science	Language/Literacy	Problem Solving	Motor Skills
• Introducing New Shapes • One to One Correspondence (count 8 sides of the Octagon)	• Vocabulary building • Describe events • Uses language in Conversation • Using Action Words in a Sentence • Developing Stories • Following Directions • Identifying Verbal Cues in a Story	• Understanding Symbols • Demonstrates Understanding of Visual and Verbal Prompts • Imagination and Creativity	• N/A

Notes: What did your child do well? Are there any skills they need to continue to work on?

B2. License Plate Name - Activity time: 15 minutes

Materials Needed:

- ☐ One (1) Piece of blank paper (any color)
- ☐ One (1) Pen
- ☐ One (1) Outdoor Area near parked vehicles.

Instructions:

Step 1: Tell your child you're going to go on a search for the letters in their name.

Step 2: The adult should write the child's name in capital letters on a blank piece of white paper.

Step 3: Tell your child to hold the pen and the piece of paper with their name on it while you go on your walk.

Step 4: Walk around the neighborhood and look at all of the license plates on vehicles. Ask your child to look for the letters that are in their name. When they see a letter on a license plate that matches a letter in their name, ask them to circle the letter on the paper.

Step 5: Continue until the child has found all the letters in their first name.

Take it to the Next Level:

1) Repeat the activity with the child's last name.

2) Repeat the activity with the child's middle name.

3) Can the child complete the activity using their full name all at once?

B.2 Learning Objectives

Math/Science	Language/Literacy	Problem Solving	Motor Skills
• N/A	• Uses language in Conversation • Following Directions • Letter Identification • Name Identification • Phonological Awareness	• Matching Letters • Searching	• Gross Motor: Walking • Fine Motor: Using a writing tool

Notes: What did your child do well? Are there any skills they need to continue to work on?

B3. Speed Limit Number March - Activity time: 20 minutes

Materials Needed:

- ☐ Four (4) Pieces of white paper
- ☐ Four (4) 3x5 index cards (any color)
- ☐ One (1) Pen

Instructions:

Step 1: The adult should use a pen to write the number "**15**" on one piece of white paper **and** one 3x5 index card.

Step 2: The adult should use a pen to write the number "**25**" on a different piece of white paper **and** a new 3x5 index card.

Step 3: The adult should use a pen to write the number "**55**" on a different piece of white paper **and** a new 3x5 index card.

Step 4: The adult should use a pen to write the number "**65**" on a different piece of white paper **and** a new 3x5 index card.

Step 5: The adult should place the four pieces of paper next to each other on the floor, in any order and in any direction.

65	25	55	15

Step 6: Show the child the 3x5 index cards with each number on it. All of these numbers are on speed limit signs. Speed limit signs tell the driver of a car how fast they can drive on the road. Tell them:

- the "**15**" represents "**slowest**" number because it is the **smallest**
- the "**65**" is the "**fastest**" number because it's the **largest.**

Step 7: Pick up a 3x5 index card, and tell your child to **march** to the piece of paper on the floor with the **same number** written on it. Once the child is **standing on the paper**, ask them to **name that number**. For example:

1. The Adult shows the child a 3x5 index card with the number "**25**" on it
2. The Child Marches over and stands on the piece of paper that has the number "**25**" on it
3. The Child says "I am standing on number "**twenty-five**".

Step 8: The adult should hold one 3x5 index card up with their **left hand** and use their **right hand** to pick another 3x5 index card. For example:

- The adult holds the 3x5 index card with the number "25" on it in their right hand.
- The adult picks another index card (with the "65" number on it) and holds it in their left hand.

| 65 | 25 |

Step 9: The child should **march** over to the piece of paper on the floor that has the same number as the 3x5 index card in the **adult's left hand.**

Step 10: Ask the child to name the number they are standing on. For example: the child will say: **"I am standing on number "65".**

Step 11: Ask the child if the number they are standing on is **faster or slower** than the first number they were standing on (the number in the adults left hand). For example:

- The adult holds the 3x5 index card with the number "25" on it in their right hand and the number "65" number in their left hand.
- The adult asks the child: "Is the number "65" **faster or slower** than the number "25"?

If the child is having a hard time answering, ask them to look at the **first numbers**. For example:

1. Number "**2**" in **25** and number "**6**" in **65**).

2. Ask the child to count to each number on their fingers (For example: count two fingers, then count six fingers).

3. Ask the child which number is bigger? Which number did you count more fingers for? (Answer: The number **6**. Six fingers.)

4. That means that the number with "**6**" as the first number (number **65**) is **faster** than the number that starts with "**2**" (number **25**) as the first number. The faster number is the larger number. The smaller number (number **25**) is **slower**.

Step 12: Repeat step 7 through Step 11 at least five more times, rotating between the four index cards.

Take it to the Next Level:

- Repeat the activity with the **second digit different**.
  - Write the numbers "10" "15" mph "30" "35"
- Repeat the activity with the **both digits different**.
  - Write the numbers "10" "25" mph "40" "65"

B.3 Learning Objectives

Math/Science	Language/Literacy	Problem Solving	Motor Skills
• Number Identification • Quantity and Counting • One to One Correspondence • Introduction to double digit numbers	• Understanding size words • Understanding descriptive words • Understanding Measurement words	• Introduction to Measurement • Using Numbers and Symbols • Understanding Opposites	• Gross Motor: Marching

Notes: What did your child do well? Are there any skills they need to continue to work on?

B4. Children's Crossing - Activity time: 20 minutes

Materials Needed:

- ☐ Three (3) Pieces of paper
- ☐ One (1) Box of Crayons
- ☐ One (1) Pen

Instructions:

Step 1: Tell your child that sometimes they will see yellow signs on the side of the road that have pictures of children on them. Those signs tell drivers of cars there may be children around and to be careful because those children might be crossing the road.

Step 2: Explain to your child that you're going to say a sentence and they're going to finish it by telling the adult where the child is crossing. They have to listen carefully!

Step 3: The adult should say the following sentence:

- Adult: "Look Out! Children are Crossing the road. They're going to the
- Child: _____(Child fills in place the children in the sign are going to)_____."

> **Example:**
> Child: the park!

Step 4: The adult should write the name of the place the child says on the bottom of one of the blank pieces of paper.

Step 5: Repeat Step 2 through 4 three more times.

Step 6: Tell the child to use crayons to draw a picture of each place they named. Each picture should be drawn on the corresponding paper with the word of the place on it.
Example:

Step 7: Ask your child what the children are going to do when they get to those places. Write what your child says on the back of the corresponding picture.

Playground 	They are going to swing, slide and play hide and seek!

B.4 Learning Objectives

Math/Science	Language/Literacy	Problem Solving	Motor Skills
• N/A	• Using words to complete phrases. • Understanding the Meaning of Words • Taking turns • Following Directions • Dictation • Imagination and Creativity	• Introduction to Syllables • Drawing Photo • Representation • Picture Identification	• Fine Motor: Using Crayons to draw a photo

Notes: What did your child do well? Are there any skills they need to continue to work on?

B5. My Street Sign - Activity time: 20 minutes

Materials Needed:

☐ One (1) Piece of Paper
☐ One (1) Black Pen
☐ One (1) Box of Crayons

Instructions:

Step 1: The adult and child should take a walk to their street corner to see their street name sign.

Step 2: Help the child read the sign to determine what their street name is. Ask them to look at the sign and name all of the letters on the sign.

Step 3: After the adult and child return home, the adult should use a pen to write the child's **street name** on a blank piece of white paper.

Step 4: Tell your child to use the box of crayons to trace the letters on the piece of paper. **The child should trace all letters that are the** same **with the same** color crayon.

For example:

- Street Name: Holland A enue

  (All the L's are Blue, All the A's are red, all the E's are green… and so on)

Step 5: Ask your child to **count the letters** that are the **same**. The adult should write **total amount** of **each letter** underneath the corresponding letter on the street name (paper from Step 4).

For Example:

H-1	N-1
O-1	D-1
L-2	
A-2	E-2
U-1	

Step 6: Ask your child to pick **one color** crayon and circle the letters that have the **same amount** in their street name.

In the example listed in Step 5:

- The child would use a blue crayon to circle the letters **A, L** and **E** because each letter has the number 2.

- They would use a green crayon to circle the letters **H, O, U, N, D** and **V** because they all have the number 1 next to them.

Step 7: Are there other street name signs near your home that you can repeat the activity with (example: cross streets or main streets)?

Learning Objectives: Letter and Word Knowledge, Letter Identification; Counting; One to One Correspondence; Identifying Colors

B.5 Learning Objectives

Math/Science	Language/Literacy	Problem Solving	Motor Skills
• Couting • Same vs. Different • One to One Correspondence	• Letter and Word Knowledge • Letter Identification • Sound/Phonological Awareness	• Word Identification • Understanding Meaning of Signs • Identifying Colors • Matching/Categorizing	• Fine Motor: Using Crayons to draw

Notes: What did your child do well? Are there any skills they need to continue to work on?

Gross Motor – Using our large muscles to move

By Completing Level 2 Activities, We will learn…

- o Uses gross motor movement skills to access a variety of obstacles and environments.
- o Hops on one foot, without support, three or more times.
- o Runs and Jumps over small objects.

Fine Motor – Using our hands to complete tasks

By Completing Level 2 Activities, We will learn…

- o Uses scissors appropriately.
- o Uses a crayon or pencil to draw or write.

C1. Freeway - Activity time: 10 minutes

Materials Needed:
☐ A large space to run

Instructions:

Step 1: Tell your child to listen to the words you are going to say. They must listen carefully so they know how **fast** they can run.

Step 2: Tell your child that when the adult says the word: **Neighborhood** – the child must **walk slowly** so they don't run into any people.

Step 3: Tell your child that when the adult says the word: **Freeway** – the child can **walk or run fast** because there are no people around.

Step 4: Ready, Set, Go! The adult should rotate back and forth between saying the words **"Neighborhood"** and **"Freeway"** and see if the child is able to **change the speed they move**.

C.1 Learning Objectives

Math/Science	Language/Literacy	Problem Solving	Motor Skills
• N/A	• Following Directions	• Understanding Measurement Concepts (Fast or Slow)	• Gross Motor: Running and Walking • Gross Motor: Balance and Coordination

Notes: What did your child do well? Are there any skills they need to continue to work on?

 **C2. Curvy Road Sign -** Activity time: 15 minutes

Materials Needed:

☐ One (1) Piece of Sidewalk Chalk
☐ One (1) Outdoor Space

Instructions:

Step 1: Tell your child that sometimes there are **signs on the side of the road that has a squiggle on it.** This means the **road is windy and curvy** and the driver must pay attention to make sure they follow **the road because it turns a lot.**

Step 2: The adult should use the sidewalk chalk to draw a very long squiggly line outdoors.

Step 3: Have the child stand on one end of the line and then **walk, stepping heal-to-toe, to the end of the line.** Did they make it or did they have to stop to regain their balance?

Need photo of heal- toe
stepping pattern

Step 4: Allow the child to make a very squiggly line with the sidewalk chalk for them to walk on (using a heal-to-toe stepping pattern).

Step 6: Repeat several times. Can the adult walk on the squiggly lines too?

C.2 Learning Objectives

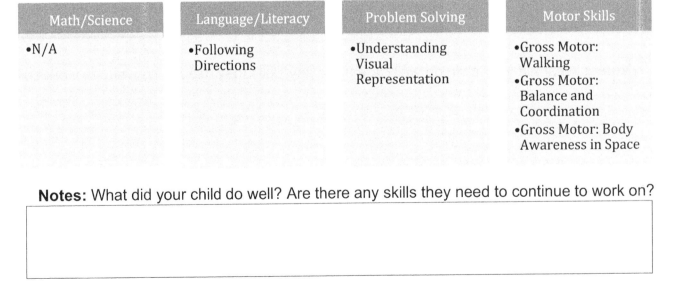

Math/Science	Language/Literacy	Problem Solving	Motor Skills
•N/A	•Following Directions	•Understanding Visual Representation	•Gross Motor: Walking •Gross Motor: Balance and Coordination •Gross Motor: Body Awareness in Space

Notes: What did your child do well? Are there any skills they need to continue to work on?

C3. Construction Zone - Activity time: 20 minutes

Materials Needed:

☐ Five (5) Orange objects (can be either paper or other objects)
☐ One (1) Roll of Painters Tape

Instructions:

Step 1: Tell your child that sometimes there is **road construction** on the side of the roads. This means **people are fixing the roads**. The workers place orange cones on the roads and wear orange vests to let drivers know to slow down. That way the cars **won't hit the workers**.

Step 2: The adult should use painters tape to make a long line on the floor. The line should be at least 8 to 10 feet long.

Step 3: Tell your child to place the 5 orange objects **next to** the taped line.

Step 5: Tell your child to jump from one end of the tape to the other. When they reach a spot near the orange objects, they must **tip toe** around them. That way they are slow and won't hit the orange paper. They're the cars and the orange objects are the road workers.

Step 6: Ready, Set, Go! When the child is done, allow them to move the orange objects to a new spot and repeat.

Step 7: Repeat Steps 4 through Step 6 as many times as they would like.

C.3 Learning Objectives

Math/Science	Language/Literacy	Problem Solving	Motor Skills
• N/A	• Following Directions • Building Vocabulary	• Understanding Visual Representation • Understanding Symbolic Colors • Identifying Colors	• Gross Motor: Jumping • Gross Motor: Balance and Coordination • Gross Motor: Body Awareness in Space • Gross Motor: Tip Toe

Notes: What did your child do well? Are there any skills they need to continue to work on?

C4. Bridges Over _____. - Activity time: 20 minutes

Materials Needed:

☐ Five (5) Objects all of different height that the child can walk or step over.

Instructions:

Step 1: Tell your child they're going to be a **bridge**. Bridges are used for cars and people to **travel over an obstacle** in a path.

Step 2: The adult should place the objects around the room.
   Examples of objects could be: empty boxes, magazines, pillows, a toy, etc.

Step 3: Tell the child to **walk AROUND** the room. When they get to an object on the floor, they are to turn into a **"BRIDGE"** and **walk OVER** the object.

Step 4: Replace the five objects with **five new objects**. Can they get over an object that is **taller** than the other ones? How tall of an object can they step over?

C.4 Learning Objectives

Math/Science	Language/Literacy	Problem Solving	Motor Skills
•N/A	•Following Directions •Building Vocabulary •Understanding Positional Words •Understanding Size Words	•N/A	•Gross Motor: Walking •Gross Motor: Balance and Coordination •Gross Motor: Body Awareness in Space

Notes: What did your child do well? Are there any skills they need to continue to work on?

C5. Through a _____ Tunnel - Activity time: 20 minutes

Materials Needed:

☐ Five (5) 3x5 Cards
☐ One (1) Pen

Instructions:

Step 1: Tell your child that its time to pretend to go on a ride! On our ride, we are going to see some tunnels! Tunnels are made so that cars can go **through** or **under** objects that are in its path.

Step 2: The adult should write the number 1 through 5 in the index cards. Only write **one number** on **each** 3x5 index card.

| 1 | 2 | 3 | 4 | 5 |

Step 3: Have the child start to walk around the room. The adult should randomly say: "Oh No! A Tunnel!"

Step 4: The adult should pick up one of the 3x5 index cards. Ask the child to **name the number** written on the card.

Step 5: Once the number has been identified, the child should get in crawling position. Tell them to crawl forward the same number of "crawls/paces" that is on the card.

For example:
If the 3x5 index card, in Step 4, said "3" then the child should crawl forward three paces – (signifying that the **tunnel is three "paces" long**).

Step 6: Repeat Steps 4 through 5 as many times as you would like, picking a new 3x5 card each time.

Step 7: Once finished, ask your child the following questions:

- Which tunnel is the longest? (Answer: 5)
- Which tunnel is the shortest? (Answer: 1)
- Which tunnel is medium length? (Answer: 3 (in the middle of 1 and 5))

Take it to the Next Level:

- Repeat the activity and ask your child to crawl **backwards.**

C.5 Learning Objectives

Math/Science	Language/Literacy	Problem Solving	Motor Skills
•Number Awareness •One to One Correspondence •Quantity and Counting •Comparing size/values	•Following Directions •Building Vocabulary •Understanding Size Words	•N/A	•Gross Motor: Crawling forwards and backwards •Gross Motor: Coordination •Gross Motor: Body Awareness in Space

Notes: What did your child do well? Are there any skills they need to continue to work on?

Pre-K YOUR Way
Level 2 Unit 3

Advanced Opposites

Unit 3: Advanced Opposites

Themed Items For Indoor Learning Environment

Now that you have set up your environment, you are ready to place materials in it that directly relate to the theme you are studying! Here are some suggestions of materials your child can free-play with during the "Advanced Opposites" Theme:

Books: Age-appropriate books that directly correlate with the monthly theme can be found at your local library or bought separately online. This is a great opportunity to take a trip with your child to your local library and go on a search together. Have them identify words or pictures on the cover of children's books that correlate to the theme. Place a variety of books related to the theme in your child's book area. This will increase opportunities for them to expand their knowledge and use what they learn in the activities to comprehend what they read in the books.

Art Area: Encourage your child use this throughout each day by rotating items in an art area. These can be items have already been painted on, paper that they drew on already or leftover materials from another project. Thought provoking art projects are created when children are given unlimited opportunities to explore a variety of materials.

Some suggestions for the art area include:
- Crayons
- Paper
- Pens
- Empty Boxes (all kinds)
- Empty Toilet Paper or Paper Towel Rolls
- Foil
- Clean Q-tips for painting
- Scraps of paper
- Scraps of Yarn
- Scraps of any type of material – including fabric, sand paper, etc.
- Paper Bags
- Straws
- Popsicle Sticks
- Anything else that can be reused.

Sensory Bin Suggestions

A sensory bin is a small plastic bucket that is filled with a variety of materials. Sensory bins provide a space to engage in sensory-rich activities that offer opportunities to investigate textures while providing activities for relaxation and self-regulation. Sensory bins encourage language development, small motor development and control, spatial concepts, problem-solving skills and scientific observations. Each month there are suggested sensory bin materials that correlate with the theme of the month.

Set Up Instructions: In a Plastic Bucket, rotate the following sensory activities throughout the month.

- **Sand Writing Table:**

Mix 2 cups of sand, 1 ½ cups cold water and 1 cup of cornstarch together. Stir the mixture for five to ten minutes over medium heat until it becomes thick. Pour the thick sand onto a cookie sheet. After it cools, have the child practice writing the Letter of the Week, writing the number of the week and drawing the Shape of the week on the sand.

Note: You can also use this mixture to build sand castles that will stick together longer.

- **Opposite Touch:**

Sensory Bins are a great time for your child to experiment different types of Touch. Place Popsicle Sticks, Small Plastic Animals and a third textured object in a Sensory Bin. Every other day, change the third item to something of a new texture. Some examples include:

  a. Sandpaper (Scratchy)
  b. Water (Wet)
  c. Play dough (Squishy)
  d. Pinecones (Hard)
  e. Crunched Leaves (Pointy/Loud)
  f. Tape (Sticky)

Dramatic Play Area

This play area allows children to understand and experience the adult world through imitation and creativity. The dramatic play area provides a safe space for young children to create stories while practicing new vocabulary and practicing social skills. It's also a space where groups of children engage in pretend play providing opportunities to learn self-help skills, share space and materials, take turns and the use abstract thinking. Each month there is a list of suggested materials to integrate into this area, which correlates with the theme of the month.

Suggested props to include in the Roadways and Signs dramatic play/pretend play area include: Tubs of Items that are Opposite.

Examples:

- Items that are Big and Small
- Items that are Soft and Hard
- Fast vs. Slow

Learning Objectives - Level 2

These activities have been developed to meet specific, age-appropriate, Kindergarten-Readiness skills. These skills are laid out in the learning objectives of each activity. The following activities may be completed in any order desired and are specifically designed to address the academic domains: math, science, language, literacy, cognitive, problem solving, and physical development. **After completing all modules in the Level 2 Curriculum Series, the child should be able to:**

Mathematics

- Identify objects by classification.
- Sort objects into categories by at least one attribute.
- Show understanding of measurement and begin to associate measurement descriptions (big, small, long, short).
- Recite numbers 1 through 10 in order.
- Count objects with one to one correspondence.
- Describe the similarities and differences of several shapes that include circle, triangle, square and rectangle.
- Create and finish simple patterns that include two elements.

Science/ Problem Solving Skills

- Develops solutions to a problem.
- Asks questions and performs simple investigations.
- Works through tasks that are difficult.
- Demonstrates understanding of visual and verbal prompts.

Language and Literacy

- Demonstrate the understanding that letters make words.
- Uses language to talk about past events.
- Uses words and increasing vocabulary to retell a story.
- Uses a variety of vocabulary to describe finding solutions to problems.
- Uses language in conversation to discover answers to questions.
- Name and match Uppercase letters.
- Accurately write all Letters of the Alphabet.
- Demonstrate Phonological Awareness of every Letter (The sounds that letters make).
- Follow simple two-step directions.

Gross Motor/Fine Motor Development

- Uses gross motor movement skills to access a variety of obstacles and environments.
- Hops on one foot, without support, three or more times.
- Runs and Jumps over small objects.
- Uses scissors appropriately.
- Uses a crayon or pencil to draw or write.

Advanced Opposites Kindergarten Readiness Themed Activities

These activities have been developed to meet specific, age-appropriate, Kindergarten-Readiness skills. These skills are specified in the learning objectives of each activity. The following activities may be completed in any order desired and are specifically designed to address the academic domains: math, science, language, literacy, cognitive, problem solving, and physical development.

Each activity is on its own page. If the adult chooses to print the activities, the space below each activity is provided for adults to write notes regarding the activity. Adults are encouraged to note if the child enjoyed the activity and if the child needs to work on specific learning objectives. Each activity can be repeated more than once to enable the child to master the learning objectives designed for that activity.

A. Math and Science Exploration
1. Heavy vs. Light
2. More vs. Less
3. Near vs. Far
4. Hot vs. Cold
5. Different vs. Same

B. Language and Literacy
1. The Sunny Day
2. Tall vs. Short Igloo Building
3. Right Side Up vs. Upside-Down
4. Stop and Go/Fast and Slow
5. The Four Seasons

C. Gross Motor and Fine Motor Activities
1. Same, Different and Similar
2. High vs. Low Jump
3. Inside and Outside Dance
4. Full vs. Empty Bucket Toss
5. Above vs. Below Contrast Art

Take it to the Next Level:

There are some activities which have a component included on how to "take an activity to the next level", increasing skill level related to the learning objectives laid out in that specific activity. Once the child has successful completed an activity, adults are encouraged to try the "take it to the next level" suggestions.

Mathematical Development – Understanding Numbers and their Purpose

By Completing Level 2 Activities, We will learn how to...
- o Identify objects by classification.
- o Sort objects into categories by at least one attribute.
- o Show understanding of measurement and begin to associate measurement descriptions (big, small, long, short).
- o Recite numbers 1 through 10 in order.
- o Count objects with one to one correspondence.
- o Describe the similarities and differences of several shapes that include circle, triangle, square and rectangle.
- o Create and finish simple patterns that include two elements.

Science/Cognitive Development – Learning How to Solve Problems

By Completing Level 2 Activities, We will learn how to..

- o Develop solutions to a problem.
- o Ask questions and performs simple investigations.
- o Work through tasks that are difficult.
- o Demonstrate understanding of visual and verbal prompts

A1. Weight Distribution – Heavy vs. Light - Activity time: 15 minutes

Materials Needed:
- One (1) kitchen food scale
- One (1) blank piece of paper
- Five (5) sea shells of different sizes.

Instructions:

Step 1: Pick **out five sea shells** that are different in **shape** and **size.**

Step 2: Place one of the shells on the kitchen scale and help the child read **how heavy** it is. Write the number (in ounces) on a piece of paper.

Step 3: Place another seashell onto the scale. Help the child read how heavy the two shells way together. Write the number (in ounces) on the piece of paper from Step 1.

Step 4: Ask the child to determine if two shells heavier than one shell?

Step 5: Add another shell to the scale and read how heavy the scale is. Write the number (in ounces) on the piece of paper from Step 1.

Step 6: Repeat Step 5 until all of the shells are added.

Step 7: Look at all of the numbers you wrote (the weight of the shells). Ask the child to identify which number is **heavier by circling it with a** green crayon? Which number is **lighter by circling it with a** blue crayon?

Take it to the Next Level:

Investigation the words: "lighter vs heavier".
Ask your child to find other objects around the home to weigh. Which objects are heavier? Which ones are lighter?

Ask the child if there are there similar characteristics to the ones that weigh heavier? How about the ones that weight lighter?

Is there a way child can make one object weigh heavier? How?

> **Example:** If they add one cup of rocks to the scale, show them that if they take one rock away, the weight is lighter. If they add another rock to the cup, it gets heavier.

A.1 Learning Objectives

Math/Science	Language	Problem Solving	Motor Skills
• Number Sense • Classification • Addition • Subtraction • One to One Correspondence • Introduction to Measurement	• Vocabulary Building • Following New Directions • Self-Expression • Language in Conversation	• Categorizing • Cause and Effect • Engagement and Persistance	• Fine Motor: Using writing materials

Notes: What did your child do well? Are there any skills they need to continue to work on?

A2. More vs. Less - Activity time: 20 minutes

Materials Needed:
- ☐ Sixteen (10) Rocks (Any Size)
- ☐ One (1) pen or pencil
- ☐ One (1) Yellow Highlighter
- ☐ One (1) Piece of Paper

Instructions:

Step 1: Ask your child if they know the difference between the words **"more"** and **"less"**.

Step 2: Help your child count the total number of rocks (Answer: 10).

Step 3: The adult should use a black marker to draw vertical a line down the middle of the blank piece of paper (shown in Step 4).

Step 4: Ask your child to place six (6) rocks on the **left side** of the paper. Tell the child to place the remaining four (4) rocks on the **right side** of the paper.

Step 5: Ask your child to count the total amount of rocks on each side of the line.

Step 6: The adult should use the yellow highlighter to write the number of rocks on the corresponding side (6 on the left side of the paper and 4 on the right). Have your child trace the numbers with a pen or pencil.

1. Rock	1. Rock
2. Rock	2. Rock
3. Rock	3. Rock
4. Rock	4. Rock
5. Rock	
6. Rock	
6	4

Step 7: Ask your child which side has **"more"** rocks, encouraging the child to point to the pile of rocks that has the most (Answer: the left side with 6 rocks).

Step 8: Ask your child which side has **"less"** rocks, encouraging the child to point to the pile of rocks that has the least (Answer: the right side with 4 rocks)

Step 9: Use a yellow highlighter to write the word **"More"** on the top of the left side of the paper, and the word **"Less"** on the top of the right side of the paper. Encourage your child to trace the words with a pen or pencil.

More	Less
1. Rock 2. Rock 3. Rock 4. Rock 5. Rock 6. Rock	1. Rock 2. Rock 3. Rock 4. Rock

Step 10: Repeat steps 4 through 8 with the following amount of Rocks:

- Place Seven (7) rocks on the left and Three (3) rocks on the right
- Place Nine (9) rocks on the left and One (1) rock on the right
- Place Eight (8) rocks on the left and Two (2) rocks on the right

Step 11: The adult should turn the piece of paper over and draw a vertical line down the middle of the paper with a black marker.

Step 12: Using a yellow highlighter write the word **"More"** on the top of the **right** side of the paper, and the word **"Less"** on the top of the **left** side of the paper.

Step 13: Encourage your child to trace the words with a pen or pencil.

Step 14: Tell your child that the words are on the **opposite sides of the paper** than in Step 10.

Step 15: Encourage the child to place **"more" rocks** on the **right** and **"less" rocks** on the **left**. Can the child identify which group is "more" and which group is "less" without looking at the words?

Less	More
1. Rock 2. Rock 3. Rock 4. Rock	1. Rock 2. Rock 3. Rock 4. Rock 5. Rock 6. Rock
4	6

Step 16: Continue working with both sides of the paper! Can your child build towers with blocks? Ask them to build a tower with "more" blocks on the side of the paper that says "more" and less blocks on the side that says "less".

A.2 Learning Objectives

Math/Science	Language	Problem Solving	Motor Skills
• Number Sense • Classification • Addition • Subtraction • One to One Correspondence • Introduction to Measurement	• Vocabulary Building • Following New Directions • Language in Conversation	• Categorizing • Engagement and Persistance	• Fine Motor: Using writing materials

Notes: What did your child do well? Are there any skills they need to continue to work on?

A3. Near vs. Far - Activity time: 15 minutes

Materials Needed
- ☐ Four (4) paper cups
- ☐ Four (4) pieces of paper
- ☐ One (1) roll of painter's tape
- ☐ One (1) yellow highlighter
- ☐ One (1) pen
- ☐ One (1) tape measure

Instructions:

Step 1: The adult should place two straight, parallel lines of painter's tape on the floor. Each line should be three feet long.

3 Feet Long

Step 2: Using a yellow highlighter, have the adult write the word **"Near"** on **two pieces** of blank paper and the word **"Far"** on **two pieces** of blank paper.

Step 3: The adult should place two paper cups on one of the "painter's tape" line, with 2 feet of space between each cup.

2 Feet

3 Feet Long

Step 4: On the other taped line, the adult should place two paper cups, six inches apart. Encourage the child to use a ruler to help measure the six-inch space between the two cups.

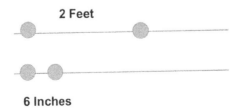

2 Feet

6 Inches

Step 5: Ask your child what set of cups is **farther** away from each other. (Answer: The cups that are 2 feet apart)

Step 6: Ask your child what set of cups is **closer** to each other. (Answer: The cups that are 6 inches apart)

Step 7: Tell your child that together, you're going to learn the words **"near"** and **"far"**.

Step 8: Have the child use a pen to copy the highlighted words, "**near**" and "**far**" on all four pieces of paper.

Step 9: Ask your child to stand on one side of the room, perpendicular to the taped lines.

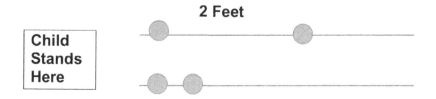

Step 10: Tell your child to point to the paper cups on each line that are "nearest" to them. Encourage the child to place the piece of paper with the word "near" written on it next to the cups that are "nearest" to the child.

Step 11: Next, encourage the child to place the piece of appear with the word "far" next to the cups that are "farthest" to the child.

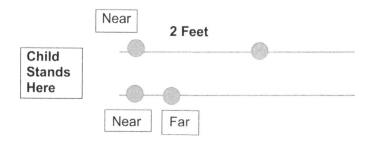

Step 12: Encourage your child to change the length of **inches** between the cups on each line to any amount of length they would like. Help them use the tape measure to find out the distance between the cups.

Step 13: Repeat steps 9 through 11.

Step 14: Ask your child if the cup closer to them or farther from them change?

Answer: No matter the space between objects, the object that is **closest** to them will always be the one that is **"near"** and the one that is **farthest** from them will always be the one that is **"far".**

Take it to the Next Level:
Have your child find two new objects that are the **same**. Have them place the items on the line and use the papers to label them "near" vs. "far".

Lesson: No matter the object, the definition of "near" and "far" won't change.

A.3 Learning Objectives

Math/Science	Language	Problem Solving	Motor Skills
• Measurement • Number Identification • Classification	• Vocabulary Building • Following Multiple-step Directions • Understanding the Meaning of Words	• Compare and Contrast • Using Tools for Problem-Solving	• Fine Motor: Using writing materials

Notes: What did your child do well? Are there any skills they need to continue to work on?

A4. Hot vs. Cold - Activity time: 15 minutes

Materials Needed
- ☐ Five (5) Pieces of **winter** clothing items (either adult or child-sized):
  - ○ Boots
  - ○ Jacket
  - ○ Long-sleeve shirt
  - ○ Long Pants
  - ○ Gloves/Mittens/Beanie/Scarf
- ☐ Five (5) Pieces of **summer** clothing items (either adult or child-sized)
  - ○ Bathing Suit
  - ○ Shorts
  - ○ Short-sleeved t-shirt
  - ○ Sandals
  - ○ Sunglasses/Visor
- ☐ Two (2) Laundry baskets

Instructions:

Step 1: While your child is not in the room, hide each of the winter and summer clothing items around a common living area (living room/kitchen/playroom). Place two empty baskets in the middle of the room.

Step 2: Tell your child they're going to go on a search for clothes to wear when it's hot and clothes to wear when it's cold.

Step 3: When they find clothes that you wear when it's hot, put them in one basket, and when they find clothes for when it's cold, put it in the other basket.

Step 4: Ready, set, Go!!!

Step 5: When they have finished ask them to count how many objects are in each pile.

Step 6: Ask your child to identify which pile has "more" and which pile has "less" (Can they remember from Activity A.2?

Step 7: Repeat the game multiple times, using a timer to see how fast they can find the items and sort them into the two piles.

Take it to the Next Level
Try completing Step 1-5 using the following clothes categories:
- Shoes vs. Sandals
- Tops vs. Bottoms
- Blue vs. All other Colors

Anything else you can think of?

A.4 Learning Objectives

Math/Science	Language	Problem Solving	Motor Skills
•Classification •One to One Correspondence	•Vocabulary Building •Following New Directions •Language in Conversation	•Memory and Knowledge •Music and Memory •Object Identification •Curiosity and Initiative •Engagement and Persistance	•N/A

Notes: What did your child do well? Are there any skills they need to continue to work on?

✎ **A5. Different vs. Same -** Activity time: 20 minutes

Materials Needed:
- ☐ Two (2) Pillows
- ☐ Two (2) Plastic Cars
- ☐ Two (2) Rocks
- ☐ Two (2) Blankets
- ☐ One (1) Box of Crayons
- ☐ Four (4) Blank Pieces of Paper

Instructions:

Step 1: Ask your child to look at the two pillows.

Step 2: Ask your child to identify what is the **same** about the two pillows.

Step 3: Ask your child to identify what is **different** about the two pillows.

Step 4: Ask your child to use crayons to draw a picture of the two pillows on one sheet of blank paper. Have them detail the photos by drawing the similarities and differences between the pillows.

Step 5: Repeat Step 1 through Step 4 using the rest of the materials from the materials list.

Take it to the Next Level:
Are there any more objects in the home that your child can find and decipher their similarities and differences?
Ask the child to go around the home and find objects that are similar, but also different. Can they identify these objects without help?

A.5 Leaning Objectives

Math/Science	Language	Problem Solving	Motor Skills
• Classification • Understanding the Concept of Two	• Vocabulary Building • Following New Directions • Langauge in Conversation • Literacy Development • Using Words to describe objects	• Color Identification • Sorting • Similar and Different	• Using a writing tool to draw

Notes: What did your child do well? Are there any skills they need to continue to work on?

Language Development – Growing our Vocabulary

By Completing Level 2 Activities, We will learn how to...
- ○ Use language to talk about past events.
- ○ Use words and increasing vocabulary to retell a story.
- ○ Use a variety of vocabulary to describe finding solutions to problems.
- ○ Use language in conversation to discover answers to questions.
- ○ Follow simple two-step directions.

Literacy Development – Beginning Reading and Writing

By Completing Level 2 Activities, We will learn how to..
- ○ Demonstrate the understanding that letters make words.
- ○ Name and match Uppercase letters.
- ○ Accurately write all Letters of the Alphabet.
- ○ Demonstrate Phonological Awareness of every Letter (The sounds that letters make).

B1. The Sunny and Cold Day - Activity time: 20 minutes

Materials Needed:
- ☐ Four (4) Blank pieces of white paper
- ☐ One (1) Set of Crayons
- ☐ One (1) Pen or pencil
- ☐ One (1) Yellow Highlighter

Instructions:

Step 1: Ask your child what items they need to have outside when it's hot?

Step 2: Encourage them to draw a picture of everything they name in Step 1.

Step 3: Ask your child to explain each item they drew and why they chose that item.

Step 4: Use a yellow highlighter to write down the name of each item that the child drew on a blank piece of paper.

Step 5: Ask your child to use a pencil to trace the words you wrote in yellow highlighter. Help him/her pronounce each letter and word as they trace the word.

Step 6: Ask your child what they would need outside when it is cold?

Step 7: Encourage them to draw a picture of each cold item on a blank piece of white paper.

Step 8: When the child is done, ask them to explain what each item is and why they chose that item.

Step 9: Use a yellow highlighter to write down the name of each item that the child drew on a blank piece of paper.

Step 10: Tell your child to use a pen to trace the words written in yellow highlighter. Help him/her pronounce each letter and word as they trace the word.

Step 11: Ask your child if they can explain why they use certain items when it is cold and other items when it's hot. This weather is opposite!

Step 12: Ask your child to count how many objects they drew on the "cold" paper and how many objects they drew on the "hot" paper. Which paper has **"more"** and which paper has **"less"**?

B.1 Learning Objectives

Math/Science	Language/Literacy	Problem Solving	Motor Skills
• One to One Correspondence	• Vocabulary building • Describe objects • Uses language in Conversation • Storytelling	• Cause and Effect • Memory and Knowledge • Creativity	• Emerging Writing • Fine Motor Development

Notes: What did your child do well? Are there any skills they need to continue to work on?

B2. Tall vs. Short Igloo Building - Activity time: 30 minutes

Materials Needed:
- ☐ Two (2) ice cube trays full of ice
- ☐ One (1) baking sheet
- ☐ One (1) paper towel
- ☐ One (1) way to access a video on the Internet.

Instructions:

Step 1 - Optional: Watch a video on YouTube about igloos in Alaska. The following YouTube video is an example: **'The Best Igloo Ever'**:
https://www.youtube.com/watch?v=pRFn4Ga2KBM

Step 2: Place one paper towel on top of a baking sheet.

Step 3: Remove the 24 ice cubes from the ice cube trays and place them on the baking sheet.

Step 4: Allow your child to build their own ice cube igloo on the tray.

Step 5: Take a picture of your child and their igloo.

Step 6: Talk about how cold the ice is when you touch it. Ask your child what they would need to stay warm if they were going to sleep in an igloo.

Step 7: Ask your child to count how many ice cubes **tall** their igloo is. The adult should write down the total number of ice cubes on the paper towel.

Step 8: Now ask your child to take their igloo apart.

Step 9: Ask your child to now build an igloo that is shorter than the one they just built (in step 4).

Step 10: Ask your child to count how many ice cubes tall the new igloo is. The adult should write down the number on the paper towel.

Step 11: Ask your child if they would rather live in the tall igloo or a short igloo? Why?

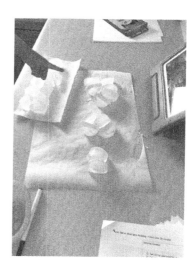

Step 12: Look at the numbers written on the paper towels.

Step 13: Ask your child to name the numbers. Ask them which number is larger than the other.

Step 14: Help your child find out the difference (how many more) ice cubes the taller igloo had. Write that number down:

Tall Igloo- 6 Ice Cubes.   **Small Igloo** – 2 Ice Cubes.   **Difference** – 4 Ice Cubes

B.2 Learning Objectives

Math/Science	Language/Literacy	Problem Solving	Motor Skills
• One to One Correspondence • Geographical Investigation • Measurement • Map Familiarization	• Vocabulary building • Describe objects • Uses language in Conversation • Folowing Multiple-Step Directions	• Cause and Effect • Memory and Knowledge • Creativity • Classification	• Emerging Writing • Fine Motor Development • Wrist Rotation and Balance

Notes: What did your child do well? Are there any skills they need to continue to work on?

B3. Right Side Up vs. Upside-Down - Activity time: 15 minutes

Materials Needed:
- ☐ Two (2) Books
- ☐ Two (2 Cups
- ☐ Two (2) Crayons
- ☐ Two (2) Cereal Boxes

Instructions:

Step 1: Tell your child you're going to find out the meaning of **Upside-Down** and **Right-side Up**.

Step 2: Place one book in front of the child that is **right side up**.

Step 3: Place the other book in front of the child that is **upside-down**.

Step 4: Ask your child to identify which one is **right side up** and which one is **upside down.**

Step 5: Repeat Steps 2 and 3 with the remaining objects.

Step 6: Now place two books in front of the child, **both right sides up**.

Step 7: Ask your child to turn one of the books **upside down**.

Step 8: Repeat Steps 6 and Step 7 with the rest of the objects.

Step 9: Now place two books in front of the child that are both **upside down**.

Step 10: Ask the child to turn one of the books **right side up**.

Step 11: Repeat step 9 and 10 with the rest of the objects.

Take it to the Next Level:
Repeat the game multiple times, using three objects that are the same:
Turn two objects upside down and place the last one right-side up.
Can your child distinguish between three objects?
How about four objects?

B.3 Learning Objectives

Math/Science	Language/Literacy	Problem Solving	Motor Skills
• One to One Correspondence • Distinguishing between Similar Characteristics	• Vocabulary building • Describe objects • Uses language in Conversation • Folowing Multiple-Step Directions	• Engagement and Persistance • Memory and Knowledge • Creativity • Classification • Curiosity and Initiative	• N/A

Notes: What did your child do well? Are there any skills they need to continue to work on?

B4. Stop and Go: Windy Races - Activity time: 20 minutes

- One (1) Stick of Sidewalk Chalk (Any Color)
- Ten (10) Craft Puff Balls (Different colors)
- One (1) Paper Plate
- One (1) Straw

Instructions:

Step 1: Using sidewalk chalk, draw two parallel, 24-inch lines, 12 inches apart from each other.

< ------------------------------24 inches--------------------------------- >

12 inches

Step 2: Ask your child: "What does it feels like when it gets windy? Can you see the wind?"

Step 3: Have your child place the Craft Pom-Pom Balls on one of the lines.

Step 4: Encourage your child to wave a paper place back and forth, making wind!

Step 5: Ask your child to use this "wind" to move the Pom-Pom craft balls from one line to the other line. Direct them to wave the paper plate directly above the Pom-Pom balls.

Step 6: Which color Pom-Pom ball crosses the other line first?

Step 7: Now have the child line all ten of the Pom-Pom balls on the line.

Step 8: Tell the child you're going to play a stop and go game.

Step 9: Tell your child they're going to have a listening game.

- When the adult says "stop", the child must stop waving the paper plate to make the wind stop.
- When the adult says "go", the child can make the wind come back by waving the plate. The goal is to move all ten Pom-Pom balls to the other line.

Step 10: The adult should say "go", wait a few seconds, then saying "stop". Repeat and change the amount of time between saying "stop" and go".

Step 11: Ask your child what they think the word **"stop"** means.

Step 12: Ask your child what they think the word **"go"** means.

Take it to the Next Level:
Repeat this activity multiple times to see how quickly it takes to get the "Pom-Pom balls" to cross the line.

Other siblings and parents can join in the fun. Who gets the Pom-Pom ball across the line first? It is a race now!

Are the children interested in creating another set of parallel lines with a larger distance between each line? Make sure they count how many "wind blows" it takes.

B.4 Learning Objectives

Math/Science	Language/Literacy	Problem Solving	Motor Skills
• One to One Correspondence • Distinguishing between Similar Characteristics	• Vocabulary building • Describe objects • Uses language in Conversation • Folowing Multiple-Step Directions	• Cause and Effect • Identifying Colors	• Fine Motor Skills: Develping a Pincer Grasp • Fine Motor Coordination

Notes: What did your child do well? Are there any skills they need to continue to work on?

B5. The Four Seasons - Activity time: 20 minutes

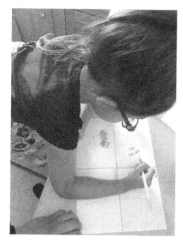

Materials Needed:
- ☐ One (1) Plain Piece of White Paper
- ☐ One (1) Set of Watercolors with paintbrush
- ☐ One (1) Black Marker
- ☐ Access to the internet

Instructions:

Step 1: Fold a white piece of paper in half, then fold it in half again.

Step 2: Open the piece of paper back up to see four areas separated by fold lines.

Step 3: Trace the fold lines with a black marker.

Step 4: Write one of the following Season words in each area:

Fall	Winter
Spring	Summer

Step 5: Tell your child that in the winter, there are **no leaves** on some trees. The adult should search for a picture of a winter tree with no leaves. A variety of photos can be found online.

Step 6: Ask your child to use the paintbrush and watercolors to paint a picture of what a tree looks like in the winter. Point to the box that says 'winter' and tell the child to paint the picture in that box.

Step 7: Repeat step 5 and 6 for each of the season boxes. (Spring – Pictures of Trees Blooming with Leaves; Summer - Pictures of Trees with Green Leaves; Fall – Pictures of Trees with Yellow, Red and Orange flowers that are falling).

Step 8: When completed, put the paper on a flat surface to dry.

B.5 Learning Objectives

Math/Science	Language/Literacy	Problem Solving	Motor Skills
• Distinguishing between Similar Characteristics	• Word Knowledge • Literacy Development • Following Directions	• Memory and Knowledge • Creativity • Classification	• Fine Motor: Painting with a Paintbrush

Notes: What did your child do well? Are there any skills they need to continue to work on?

Gross Motor – Using our large muscles to move

> **By Completing Level 2 Activities, We will learn…**
> - Uses gross motor movement skills to access a variety of obstacles and environments.
> - Hops on one foot, without support, three or more times.
> - Runs and Jumps over small objects.

Fine Motor – Using our hands to complete tasks

> **By Completing Level 2 Activities, We will learn…**
>
> - Uses scissors appropriately.
> - Uses a crayon or pencil to draw or write.

C1. Same, Different and Similar - Activity time: 20 minutes

Materials Needed:

☐ One (1) Roll of Painter's Tape
☐ Five (5) Red pieces of paper
☐ Five (5) Blue pieces of paper
☐ One (1) Pair of Adult-sized Scissors

Instructions:

Step 1: The adult should use scissors to cut-out **four, same-sized circles**, out of two blue pieces of paper.

Step 2: The adult should use the scissors to cut-out out **four, same-sized circles**, out of two red blue pieces of paper.

Step 3: The adult should use the scissors to cut-out **four, same-sized squares**, out of two blue pieces of paper.

Step 4: The adult should use the scissors to cut-out **four, same-sized squares**, out of two red pieces of paper.

Step 5: The adult should use the painters tape to make three equal sized circles. Each circle should be at least 24 inches in diameter. The three circles should be placed in a straight, horizontal line – one circle right next to another.

Step 6: The adult should tell the child they're going to sort the shapes into groups of the "same", "different" and "similar".

Step 7: Have the child put all the blue circles inside one taped circle. Tell them all of the blue circles are the same.

Step 8: Now have the child put all the red circles in a different taped circle. Tell the child these red circles are different then the blue circles. Can they tell the adult why they are different?

Step 9: Now have the child put one blue circle and one blue square in the last taped circle. Tell the child that these two are similar. Can the child tell you why? (Answer: they are both the color blue).

Step 10: Ask your child what makes the blue circles and the red circles the **same**? (Answer: They are the same shape.)

Step 11: Ask the child what makes the blue square **different** then the blue circles? (Answer: They have different amounts of side).

Step 12: Ask the child what makes the blue circle and the blue square **similar** (Answer: They are both blue)?

Step 13: Now have your child jump inside the circle that corresponds with the following directions from the adult:

    A) "Jump into the circles with the objects that are the **same**"
    B) "Jump into the circles with the objects that are **different**"

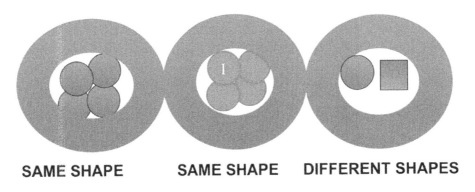

    SAME SHAPE   SAME SHAPE   DIFFERENT SHAPES

Step 14: Ask your child to place all the red circles in one circle (same).

Step 15: Have your child place all the blue circles in the next circle (they are different than the red circles).

Step 16. Ask your child to place one blue circle and one red circle in the last circle (similar).

Step 17: Ask your child: " Why are the blue circles and the red circles are **similar**?" (Answer: They are both circles.)

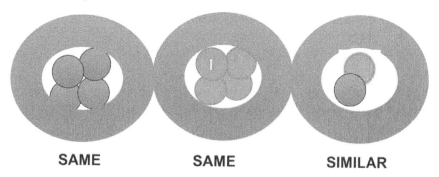

SAME   SAME   SIMILAR

Step 18: Now have the child complete the following directions:

    A) "Jump onto the shapes that are the **same**."
    B) "Jump onto the shapes are **similar**."

Step 19: Repeat step 18, but change up the order of the directions. Say the directions fast, then say the directions slow. How fast can the child jump from one circle to the other?

Step 20: Now Repeat steps 7 through 13 using the red and blue squares instead of the circles.

Step 21: Ask your child to place all the blue squares in one circle.

Step 22: Ask your child to place all the blue circle in another circle.

Step 23: Ask your child to place one blue square and one blue circle in the last circle.

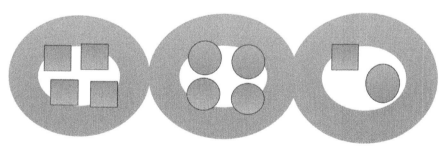

Step 24: Ask your child: "What makes these objects the **same**?" (Answer: Both the circle and square are blue.)

Step 25: Ask your child: "What makes these objects **different**?" (Answer: The Circle has zero sides and square has four sides.)

Step 26: Repeat step 18, but change up the order of the directions. Say the directions fast, then say the directions slow. How fast can the child jump from one circle to the other?

Take it to the Next Level:

Repeat this activity multiple times using the following options:

A) **Circle 1:** Red square, **Circle 2:** Red Circle, **Circle 3:** one red circle and one red square.

B) Have your child find other objects around the house that are similar. Place them in the corresponding circles. What makes them similar and different?

C.1 Learning Objectives

Math/Science	Language/Literacy	Problem Solving	Motor Skills
• Sorting • Similar vs. Different • Organization • One to One Correspondence	• Following Directions	• Identifying Colors • Identifying Shapes	• Gross Motor: Jumping • Gross Motor: Balance and Coordination

Notes: What did your child do well? Are there any skills they need to continue to work on?

Materials Needed:

☐ One (1) Roll of Painter's Tape
☐ One (1) Step stool (or the bottom stair of a staircase)

Instructions:

Step 1: The adult should place one small 6-inch line of painter's tape on the floor.

Step 2: Ask the child to demonstrate how they stand on one foot.

Step 3: Now ask the child to hop on one foot, counting how many times they can hop.

Step 4: Have the child hop, on one foot, over the taped line on the floor.

Over

Step 5: Have the child stand on top of the step stool, or bottom stair of a staircase, near the taped line on the floor.

Step 6: Ask the child if they are **higher** or **lower** than the blue line (Answer: **Higher**).

Step 7: Have the child jump from the top of the first step to the floor, landing on two feet.

Step 8: Now ask the child if they are **higher** or **lower** then when they were standing on the step (Answer: **Lower**).

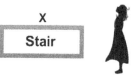

X

Stair

Step 9: Ask the child to hop, **on one foot**, over the taped line. Are they **higher** or **lower** then when they were standing on the step (Answer: **Lower**).

Step 10: Tell the child that you are going to play a game called **Jump vs. Hop.**

Step 11: Tell your child that when you say **"Jump"**, they are to **jump off the bottom stair** or step stool **and land on two feet**. When they jump, they need to say the word **"High"**. They will be higher than the floor.

Step 12: Tell the child that when you **say "Hop"**, they need to **hop, on one foot, over** the painter's tape and **say "Low"**. They will be lower than the step.

Step 13: Ready, set, go! Have the adult say the following pattern sequences, having the child follow the directions in step 11:

    A. "Jump," "Jump", "Hop", "Jump", "Jump", "Hop", "Jump", "Jump, "Hop"

    B. "Hop". "Hop", "Hop", "Jump", "Jump", "Hop", "Hop", "Hop", "Jump", "Jump", "

    B. Jump", "Hop", "Jump", "Hop", "Jump", "Hop"

    C. Can the child come up with some more patterns?

C.2 Learning Objectives

Math/Science	Language/Literacy	Problem Solving	Motor Skills
•Understanding Size Words •Understanding Patterns	•Following Directions •Develop New Vocabulary •Describing Words	•Understanding Spacial Concepts	•Gross Motor: Jumping •Gross Motor: Hopping on One Foot •Gross Motor: Balance and Coordination

Notes: What did your child do well? Are there any skills they need to continue to work on?

C3. Inside and Outside Dance - Activity time: 10 minutes

Materials Needed:

☐ One (1) Empty Cardboard Box, large enough for the child to sit inside
☐ Four (4) Pieces of paper
☐ One (1) Black Marker

Instructions:

Step 1: The adult should put an empty cardboard box on the floor.

Step 2: The adult should write the number "1" on one piece of paper and the number "2" on the other piece of paper.

Step 3: Tell your child: "When I hold up the paper with the **number "1"** on it, **sit down inside the box."**

Step 4: Tell the child: When I hold up the **number "2"** on it, **get out of the box and dance."**

Step 5: Hold up the **number "1".** Once the child sits inside the box, the adult should say: " Wonderful! You are **"inside"** the box."

Step 6: Hold up the **number 2**. Once the child gets out of the box, the adult should say: "Great! You are **"outside"** of the box. Let's dance!"

Step 7: Ready, set, go! Hold up the pieces of paper with the corresponding number on it, in the order typed below. Complete the following pattern sequence, having the child follow the directions in step 5 and 6 when you hold up the number.

- 1,1,2,1,1,2

- 2,2,1,2,2,1

- 1,2,1,2,1,2,1

- 2,1,2,1,2,1,2

- 2,2,2,1,2,2,2,1

- 1,1,2,2,1,1,2,2

- 2,1,1,2,2,

- 1,2,2,1,1

Step 8: Repeat and increase the speed in which the signs are held.

Step 9: Change spots with the child and have the adult follow the number directions.

Take it to the Next Level:

Step 10: Can your child come up with some more things they can do inside the box (spin in a circle, jump, stand on one foot, etc)?

Step 11. The adult should write the number "3" on a new piece of paper. Have the child pick what movement they want to do in the box when they see the number "3".

Step 12: Can your child come up with some more things they can do outside the box (shake, wiggle, run, lay down, etc)?

Step 13: The adult should write the number "4" on a new piece of paper. Have the child pick what movement they want to do outside of the box when they see the number "4".

Step 14: The adult should hold up the pieces of paper in the following sequence. Ask the child follow the directions in step 5 and 6, adding in the actions they chose for number "3" and number "4".

A.	1,2,3,1,2,3
B.	2,3,4,2,3,4
C.	1,3,4,1,3,4
D.	1,1,2,2,3,3,4,4
E.	4,4,3,3,4,4,3,3,
F.	4,3,3,3,3,4,3,3,3,3,
G.	2,4,4,2,4,4
H.	1,1,3,3,1,1,3,3
I.	2,1,3,2,1,3

    – Make sure to continue increasing the rate of speed when switching between the numbers.

Step 15: Change spots with the child and have the adult follow the number directions.

Step 16: Can your child think up more patterns with these numbers and actions?

C.3 Learning Objectives

Math/Science	Language/Literacy	Problem Solving	Motor Skills
•Understanding Patterns •Creating New Patterns •Number Idetification	•Following Directions •Develop New Vocabulary •Describing Words	•Understanding Spacial Concepts •Understanding Symbol Identification	•Gross Motor: Climbing •Gross Motor: Dancing •Gross Motor: Balance and Coordination •Movement skills to access a variety of obstacles

Notes: What did your child do well? Are there any skills they need to continue to work on?

C4. Full vs. Empty Bucket Toss - Activity time: 10 minutes

Materials Needed:
- ☐ One (1) Empty Shoebox
- ☐ Ten (10) Small balls OR Ten (10) pieces of scratch paper crumbled into ten small balls.

Instructions:

Step 1: The adult should put an empty shoebox on the floor. Tell your child you're going to talk about the difference between **full vs. empty.**

Step 2: Tell your child to throw **all of the balls** into the shoebox, **counting each ball** they throw (1 through 10).

Step 3: Once all of the balls are in the box, ask the child if the shoebox is **full or empty** (**Answer: full).** Ask them why they think it is full (**Answer: Because there are items in the box and there is no more room to put anymore inside).**

Step 4: Now, ask your child to dump **all of the balls out of the box**. Ask the child if the box is **empty or full** (**Answer: It is empty because there are no balls in it).**

Step 5: Next, the adult should ask the child **what they think the opposite of full is**? (Answer: Empty)

Step 6: Next, the adult should ask the child **what they think the opposite of empty is**? (Answer: Full)

C.4 Learning Objectives

Math/Science	Language/Literacy	Problem Solving	Motor Skills
•Understanding Quantity Words •Number Identification	•Following Directions •Develop New Vocabulary •Describing Words	•Understanding Spacial Concepts	•Gross Motor: Throwing •Gross Motor: Dumping

Notes: What did your child do well? Are there any skills they need to continue to work on?

C5 Above vs. Below Contrast Art - Activity time: 10 minutes

Materials Needed:
- ☐ One (1) Piece of blank paper
- ☐ One (1) Black Pen
- ☐ One (1) Pair of child-safe scissors
- ☐ Three (3) Grocery Store Sale papers
- ☐ One (1) Glue stick

Instructions:

Step 1: The adult should draw a horizontal line across the middle of the blank piece of paper.

Step 2: Tell the child they're going to cut out **each vegetable** and **each fruit** that's in the grocery store sale papers. Encourage them to use child-safe scissors to cut out each one individually.

Step 3: Once the child has cut out all of the pictures, tell the child to glue all of the **pictures of fruit above the line** on the piece of paper.

Step 4: Next, tell the child to glue all of the pictures of the **vegetables below the line** on the piece of paper.

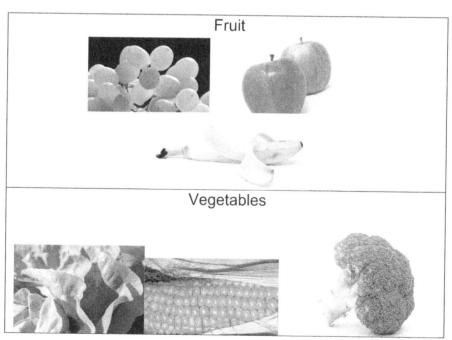

Step 5: Describe each of the foods now that they are sorted into **categories. The fruit is above the line and the vegetables are below the line.**

Take it to the Next Level:

Ask your child if there are other items in the grocery store sale paper they want to cut out and sort by categories (cleaning products, paper products, meat products, dairy products, pet products).

On another piece of paper, the adult can draw a horizontal line and have the child sort the items by category, choosing one category for **"above"** and one category for **"below"** the line.

C.5 Learning Objectives

Math/Science	Language/Literacy	Problem Solving	Motor Skills
•N/A	•Following Directions •Develop New Vocabulary •Describing Words	•Understanding Spacial Concepts •Identifying Categories •Classification	•Fine Motor: Using Scissors •Fine Motor: Glue

Notes: What did your child do well? Are there any skills they need to continue to work on?

Pre-K YOUR Way

Level 2 Unit 4

Exploring My Home

Unit 4: My Home

Themed Items For Indoor Learning Environment

Now that you have set up your environment, you are ready to place materials in it that directly relate to the theme you are studying! Here are some suggestions of materials your child can free-play with during the "My Home" Theme:

Books: Age-appropriate books that directly correlate with the monthly theme can be found at your local library or bought separately online. This is a great opportunity to take a trip with your child to your local library and go on a search together. Have them identify words or pictures on the cover of children's books that correlate to the theme. Place a variety of books related to the theme in your child's book area. This will increase opportunities for them to expand their knowledge and use what they learn in the activities to comprehend what they read in the books.

Art Area: Encourage your child use this throughout each day by rotating items in an art area. These can be items have already been painted on, paper that they drew on already or leftover materials from another project. Thought provoking art projects are created when children are given unlimited opportunities to explore a variety of materials.

Some suggestions for the art area include:
- Crayons
- Paper
- Pens
- Empty Boxes (all kinds)
- Empty Toilet Paper or Paper Towel Rolls
- Foil
- Clean Q-tips for painting
- Scraps of paper
- Scraps of Yarn
- Scraps of any type of material – including fabric, sand paper, etc.
- Paper Bags
- Straws
- Popsicle Sticks
- Anything else that can be reused.

Sensory Bin Suggestions

A sensory bin is a small plastic bucket that is filled with a variety of materials. Sensory bins provide a space to engage in sensory-rich activities that offer opportunities to investigate textures while providing activities for relaxation and self-regulation. Sensory bins encourage language development, small motor development and control, spatial concepts, problem-solving skills and scientific observations. Each module includes a suggested sensory bin materials that correlate with the theme.

Set Up Instructions: In a Plastic Bucket, rotate the following sensory activities throughout the month.

- **Sand Writing Table:**
  Mix 2 cups of sand, 1 ½ cups cold water and 1 cup of cornstarch together. Stir the mixture for five to ten minutes over medium heat until it becomes thick. Pour the thick sand onto a cookie sheet. After it cools, have the child practice writing the Letter of the Week, writing the number of the week and drawing the Shape of the week on the sand.

  Note: You can also use this mixture to build sand castles that will stick together longer.

- **Foil Homes:**
  Homes are all different colors and shapes and sizes. Place some popsicle sticks and some sheets of foil into the sensory bin. When the child is ready to play with the sensory bin, allow them to use water based, non-toxic finger-paint, to paint sheets of foil. They can then use the popsicle sticks and colored foil to build a variety of shaped houses.

Dramatic Play Area

This play area allows children to understand and experience the adult world through imitation and creativity. The dramatic play area provides a safe space for young children to create stories while practicing new vocabulary and practicing social skills. It's also a space where groups of children engage in pretend play providing opportunities to learn self-help skills, share space and materials, take turns and the use abstract thinking. Each month there is a list of suggested materials to integrate into this area, which correlates with the theme.

Suggested props to include in the dramatic play/pretend play area include:

- A piece of cardboard, long enough for the child to lay down on.
- Blanket or Sheet
- Pillows
- Plastic silverware
- Paper Plates
- Paper Cups
- Pretend food
- Empty Cereal Boxes and other food boxes
- A child sized chair
- A Large Empty Box (could be a bed, a table, a bathtub, a sink, etc)
- Markers for Boxes
- Baby dolls
- Baby doll clothes
- Child's clothes and Empty Boxes for closet/drawers
- Anything else the child can think she/he may need in their play home?

Learning Objectives - Level 2

These activities have been developed to meet specific, age-appropriate, Kindergarten-Readiness skills. These skills are laid out in the learning objectives of each activity. The following activities may be completed in any order desired and are specifically designed to address the academic domains: math, science, language, literacy, cognitive, problem solving, and physical development. **After completing all modules in the Level 2 Curriculum Series, the child should be able to:**

Mathematics

- Identify objects by classification.
- Sort objects into categories by at least one attribute.
- Show understanding of measurement and begin to associate measurement descriptions (big, small, long, short).
- Recite numbers 1 through 10 in order.
- Count objects with one to one correspondence.
- Describe the similarities and differences of several shapes that include circle, triangle, square and rectangle.
- Create and finish simple patterns that include two elements.

Science/ Problem Solving Skills

- Develops solutions to a problem.
- Asks questions and performs simple investigations.
- Works through tasks that are difficult.
- Demonstrates understanding of visual and verbal prompts.

Language and Literacy

- Demonstrate the understanding that letters make words.
- Uses language to talk about past events.
- Uses words and increasing vocabulary to retell a story.
- Uses a variety of vocabulary to describe finding solutions to problems.
- Uses language in conversation to discover answers to questions.
- Name and match Uppercase letters.
- Accurately write all Letters of the Alphabet.
- Demonstrate Phonological Awareness of every Letter (The sounds that letters make).
- Follow simple two-step directions.

Gross Motor/Fine Motor Development

- Uses gross motor movement skills to access a variety of obstacles and environments.
- Hops on one foot, without support, three or more times.
- Runs and Jumps over small objects.
- Uses scissors appropriately.
- Uses a crayon or pencil to draw or write

My Home and Beyond Themed Academic Activities

These activities were developed to meet specific, age-appropriate, Kindergarten-Readiness skills. These skills are specified in the learning objectives of each activity. The following activities may be completed in any order desired and are specifically designed to address the academic domains: math, science, language, literacy, cognitive, problem solving, and physical development.

Each activity is on its own page. If the adult chooses to print out the activities, the space below each activity is provided for adults to write notes regarding the activity. Adults are encouraged to note if the child enjoyed the activity and if the child needs to work on specific learning objectives. Each activity can be repeated more than once to enable the child to master the learning objectives designed for that activity.

A. Math/Science Development....pg. 11-22
1. Building Tools
2. Measurements and their Purpose
3. Shape Classification
4. Construction Numbers
5. Big or Small

B. Language/Literacy Development....pg. 23-35
1. In a Great Big House
2. I opened the Door and _____.
3. Animal Home Match
4. HOME hunt
5. Rooms and their things

C. Physical Development- Gross Motor & Fine-Motor....pg.36-47
1. Up on the Rooftop
2. Stairs or No Stairs
3. 1 floor, 2 floors, 3 floors, More?
4. Direction Maze
5. Kitchen Jump

Take it to the Next Level:
There are some activities which have a component included on how to "take an activity to the next level", increasing skill level related to the learning objectives laid out in that specific activity. Once the child has successful completed an activity, adults are encouraged to try the "take it to the next level" suggestions.

Mathematical Development – Understanding Numbers and their Purpose

By Completing Level 2 Activities, We will learn how to...

- o Identify objects by classification.
- o Sort objects into categories by at least one attribute.
- o Show understanding of measurement and begin to associate measurement descriptions (big, small, long, short).
- o Recite numbers 1 through 10 in order.
- o Count objects with one to one correspondence.
- o Describe the similarities and differences of several shapes that include circle, triangle, square and rectangle.
- o Create and finish simple patterns that include two elements.

Science/Cognitive Development – Learning How to Solve Problems

By Completing Level 2 Activities, We will learn how to..

- o Develop solutions to a problem.
- o Ask questions and performs simple investigations.
- o Work through tasks that are difficult.
- o Demonstrate understanding of visual and verbal prompts

A1. Building Tools - Activity time: 30 minutes

Materials Needed:

☐ One (1) or Two (2) Home Improvement Store Sale Papers
☐ One (1) Pair of Child-safe scissors
☐ One (1) Black Marker
☐ One (1) Blank Pieces of White Paper
☐ One (1) Glue Stick
☐ One (1) Yellow Highlighter

Instructions:

Step 1: Gather one or two Home Improvement store sale papers. Put them on a table near your child.

Step 2: Ask your child to look through the sale papers and cut out pictures of tools they find.

Step 3: Once they have finished cutting out the pictures, tell them to place the pictures in front of them.

Step 4: Ask them to identify what each tool is. Do they know the names of them?

Step 5: Ask your child to count how many tools they found.

Step 6: The adult should use a yellow highlighter to write the word "Tools" in the middle of a blank sheet of paper.

Step 7: Using the glue stick, have your child glue the pictures of all the tools they cut out on the paper around the word "Tools".

Step 8: Using a pen or pencil, encourage the child to trace the word "Tools" that is written in the middle of the page.

A.1 Learning Objectives

Math/Science	Language	Problem Solving	Motor Skills
• Number Sense • One to One Correspondence • Mathematical Operations	• Following New Directions • Expression of Self	• Search and Identify • Categorization	• Fine Motor: Using Scissors • Fine Motor: Tracing

Notes: What did your child do well? Are there any skills they need to continue to work on?

A2. Measurements and their Purpose - Activity time: 15 minutes

Materials Needed:

☐ One (1) Tape Measure
☐ Two (2) Sheets of Blank, White Paper
☐ One (1) Pen
☐ One (1) Ruler

Instructions:

*** Caution – Automatic retracting tape measures can be hazardous and can cut and injure. Use caution if using one of the tape measures and maintain close supervision of the child.

Step 1: Have your child pick one room in your home they would like to measure.

Step 2: Using a measuring tape, ask your child hold one end of the tape and the adult should hold the other side. Measure the length of each wall of the room.

Step 3: The adult should write down the number (in feet) of the size of each wall on a white piece of paper.

Step 4: After all walls have been measured, place a blank piece of paper and a ruler in front of the child.

Step 5: Show the child the inch marks on the ruler. Tell the child that each inch mark will "represent" one foot. **Example:**

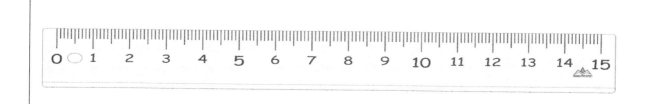

7 Inches = 7 feet

Step 6: Looking at the length (in feet) of the walls that were measured in Step 3. Ask the child to count the same number of inches on the ruler.

Step 7: Have the child draw one line to represent each wall they measured.

Step 8: Next to each line "wall" the adult should write down the number of inches that correspond to each wall. **Example:**

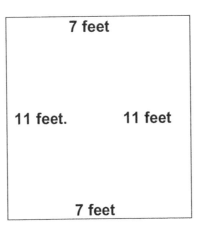

Step 9: Ask your child to look at the length of each wall. Ask your child the following questions:

- Which wall is the longest?
- Are there any walls that are the same size?

Take it to the Next Level:

Measure other rooms in the house and repeat steps 3 through 7.

Ask your child the following questions:

- Which room in the home is bigger?
- Which room in the home is smaller?

A.2 Learning Objectives

Math/Science

- Number Sense
- Measurement
- Classification
- One to One Correspondence
- Mathematical Operations

Language

- Following New Directions
- Increasing Vocabulary

Problem Solving

- Engagement and Persistence
- Curiosity and Initiative
- Symbol Knowledge
- Identifying Shapes
- Compare and Contrast

Motor Skills

- Fine Motor: Using Writing Tools

Notes: What did your child do well? Are there any skills they need to continue to work on?

A3. Building Shapes - Activity time: 20 minutes

Materials Needed:

☐ Four (4) sheets of blank construction paper (any color)
☐ One (1) Black Marker
☐ One (1) Pair of adult scissors
☐ Twenty (2) Popsicle Sticks
☐ One (1) Roll of Scotch Tape
☐ Pictures in a book or on the internet of different buildings

Instructions:

Step 1: On one piece of construction paper, the adult should use a black marker to draw **two circles** that are the same size.

Step 2: On the second piece of construction paper draw **two triangles** that are the same size.

Step 3: On the third piece of construction paper, draw **two rectangles** that are the same size.

Step 4: On the fourth piece of construction paper, draw **two squares** that are the same size.

Step 5: Next, the adult should cut out each shape.

Step 6: Mix up all of the shapes together.

Step 7: Have your child sit at a table, placing the shapes in front of them. Ask them to sort the shapes into similar piles (all squares together, all triangles together, all circles together and all rectangles together).

Step 8: Once the shapes have been sorted, ask your child what each shape is? Ask your child if they can identify two or three different facts about each shape.

> **Example:** "The square has four sides.
> The square has four sides that are all the same size.
> Both of these squares are Red."

Step 9: Tell your child they're going to create some buildings with these shapes using popsicle sticks and some tape. Allow them to create any building they want.

Step 10: Show your child all of the pictures of different buildings.

Step 11: Ask your child to identify what building they just made and describe each part of the building to you. What shapes did they choose to make their building? What does each shape represent (door, floor, design, etc). **Example:**

Circle = Window
Square = House
Triangle = Roof
Rectangle= door

A.3 Learning Objectives

Math/Science	Language	Problem Solving	Motor Skills
• One to One Correspondence • Categorizing	• Following New Directions • Expression of Self • Explaining Details	• Identifying Shapes • Sorting • Matching	• Fine Motor: Using Hands to Complete Tasks

Notes: What did your child do well? Are there any skills they need to continue to work on?

A4. Construction Numbers - Activity time: 20 minutes

Materials Needed:

- ☐ One (1) Piece of Sidewalk Chalk
- ☐ One (1) Tape Measure
- ☐ One (1) Piece of Blank Paper
- ☐ One (1) Camera or Access to a Camera App (smart phone or tablet)
- ☐ One (1) Pen

Instructions:

Caution – Automatic retracting tape measures can be hazardous and can cut and injure. Use caution if using one of the tape measures and maintain close supervision of the child.

Step 1: Tell your child they're going to be able to make their own house or building.

Step 2: Tell your child to decide how many walls they want their home to have. On a concrete surface, allow your child use a measuring tape to **measure the length of each wall** for their home.

Step 3: Help your child draw each line (wall) with sidewalk chalk.

Step 4: Show your child where the number (in feet) is located on the measuring tape.

Step 5: Encourage them to write that number next to each wall they draw so they can remember how long it is. If they're having trouble writing the number, the adult can write the number for them and have the child trace the number.

Step 6: Continue step 3 and 4 until the entire building has been drawn.

Step 7: Ask the child what they built? Who lives in the building?

Step 8: Take a picture of the "building" plan that your child created.

Step 9: Ask your child to tell you a story about who lives in the building. Write what the child says on a blank piece of paper.

Step 10: Print the photo you took of the child's plan (from Step 8) and attach it to their story they told you.

A.4 Learning Objectives

Math/Science	Language	Problem Solving	Motor Skills
•One to One Correspondence •Number Identification •Utilizing Measuring Tools, •Quantity and Counting	•Following New Directions •Expression of Self •Size word Identification •Dictation •Concepts of Print •Emerging Writing •Expressions of Self through Language •Interest in Literacy	•Categorizing •Comprehension of Meaning •Socio-Dramatic Play •Buiding Relationsihps	•Fine Motor: Using Hands to Complete Tasks

Notes: What did your child do well? Are there any skills they need to continue to work on?

A5. Big or Small? - Activity time: 20 minutes

Materials Needed:

☐ Two (2) Pieces of Blank White Paper
☐ One (1) Blue Marker
☐ One (1) Red Marker
☐ One (1) Ruler

Instructions:

Step 1: The adult should use a blue marker to write down the word **"BIG"** on a blank piece of paper.

Step 2: The adult should use a red marker to write down the word **"SMALL"** on a blank piece of paper.

Step 3: Tell your child they're going to go on a scavenger hunt around your house to find items that are **big and small**.

Step 4: For this game, **anything that is under 6 inches will be categorized as "small"** and **anything over 6 inches will be categorized as "big".**

Step 5: Show your child the ruler. Help your child identify where the "6" is on the ruler.

Step 6: Tell your child they have **two minutes** to find as many items as they can and place them into **a "BIG" pile and a "SMALL" pile.**

Step 7: Set a timer **for two minutes and ... GO!**

Step 8: Once the timer is off, ask your child to stand by the piles of items they found.

Step 9: Ask them to look at the ruler and show you where the number 6 is.

Step. 10: Tell them that anything bigger or longer then "6" inches will be put next to the **BIG sign,** while anything under 6 inches will be put next to the **SMALL sign**.

Step 11: The adult should help the child measure each object and categorize them appropriately (big or small).

Step 12: Ask your child to count how many items are in each category. The adult should write the total number of small items on the paper that says SMALL (from step 2), and the total number of big items on the paper that says BIG (from Step 1).

Step 13: Clean up time! The adult should set the timer for two minutes and see if your child can put all the objects they found back in their appropriate spots before the timer goes off.

A.5 Learning Objectives

Math/Science	Language	Problem Solving	Motor Skills
• One to One Correspondence • Categorizing • Introduction to Measurement	• Following New Directions • Explaining Details • Letter and Word Knowledge • Using Language in Conversations	• Classification • Sorting • Matching	• Fine Motor: Using Hands to Complete Tasks

Notes: What did your child do well? Are there any skills they need to continue to work on?

Language Development – Growing our Vocabulary

By Completing Level 2 Activities, We will learn how to...

- ○ Use language to talk about past events.
- ○ Use words and increasing vocabulary to retell a story.
- ○ Use a variety of vocabulary to describe finding solutions to problems.
- ○ Use language in conversation to discover answers to questions.
- ○ Follow simple two-step directions.

Literacy Development – Beginning Reading and Writing

By Completing Level 2 Activities, We will learn how to..

- ○ Demonstrate the understanding that letters make words.
- ○ Name and match Uppercase letters.
- ○ Accurately write all Letters of the Alphabet.
- ○ Demonstrate Phonological Awareness of every Letter (The sounds that letters make).

B1. In A Great BIG House - Activity time: 30 minutes

Materials Needed:

☐ Two (2) Blank Pieces of Paper
☐ One (1) Pen
☐ One (1) Box of Crayons

Instructions:

Step 1: The adult should write the word **"BIG"**, in capital letters, on the top on one piece of blank paper.

Step 2: Tell your child that it's their job to draw a great **"BIG"** house on the sheet of paper using crayons.

Step 3: When your child is done drawing a picture, the adult should write the following words on another sheet of blank paper:

- People
- Bedrooms
- Bathrooms
- Kitchens
- Stairs
- Colors

Step 4: Ask your child how many of each room (listed in Step 3) is in the **"BIG"** house they drew in Step 2. The adult should write the numbers next to each room from Step 3.

Example: Bedrooms: 11111 (if the child says 5 bedrooms).

Step 5: When completed, ask the child what colors are in their house. The adult should use the crayons of those colors to write the words

Example: Colors: Red Blue   Green

Step 6: When completed, show your child the numbers next to each room. Tell them to make the same amount of tally marks for each number.

Example:
- Bathrooms 111 = 3
- Kitchens 11 = 2

- **Step 7:** Next, have your child trace the numbers with a crayon color of their choice.

Take it to the Next Level:

Ask the child if there are any other rooms in the house they drew. Repeat step 3 through 8 asking them about the additional rooms.

B.1 Learning Objectives

Math/Science	Language/Literacy	Problem Solving	Motor Skills
•Introducing New Shapes •One to One Correspondence (count 8 sides of the Octagon) •Quantity and Counting	•Vocabulary building • Imagination and Creativity •Using Words to Form Ideas •Letter Identification Understanding the Letters make Words	• Imagination and Creativity	•Fine Motor: Using Writing Tools

Notes: What did your child do well? Are there any skills they need to continue to work on?

B2. I Opened the Door AND _____. - Activity time: 15 minutes

Materials Needed:

☐ One (1) Piece of Cardboard
  (At least 2 feet tall and 2 feet wide)
☐ Two (2) Empty Shoeboxes

Instructions:

Step 1: Give your child an empty shoebox and tell them they can put four objects of their choosing into the box. Tell them to make sure they put the lid on top before they bring the box back.

Step 2: The adult should also fill up a shoebox with four objects of their choosing, placing the lid back on the box so the child can't see what's inside.

Step 3: The adult and child should sit across from each other placing the piece of cardboard in the middle, separating them (so they can't see each other's shoe boxes).

Step 4: The adult should take one object out of the box and place it on top of their shoe box, behind the cardboard, so the child doesn't see it.

Step 5: Tell the child that the piece of cardboard is actually a "door". We are going to play a peek-a-boo game!

Step 6: The adult will start by knocking on the cardboard, saying, "knock, knock."

Step 7: Tell the child to repeat the following phrase:

"I heard a knock. I opened the door and __(object)_ was there!"

Have the child state the name of the hidden object the adult placed on top of the shoebox.

Step 8: Now it's the child's turn. The child should take one object out of the box and place it on their side of the piece of cardboard so the adult doesn't see it.

Step 9: The child will start by knocking on the cardboard saying, "knock, knock."

Step 10: The adult should say:

"I heard a knock. I opened the door and __(object)_ was there!"

Have the adult state the name of the hidden object the child placed behind the cardboard.

Step 11: Repeat steps 4 through 10 until both the adult and the child see all 8 objects.

Step 12: Play again! Go find four more objects to hide!

B.2 Learning Objectives

Math/Science	Language/Literacy	Problem Solving	Motor Skills
• One to One Correspondence • Quantity and Counting	• Vocabulary building • Imagination and Creativity • Using Words to Form a Sentence	• Imagination and Creativity • Turn Taking • Repetition • Socio-dramatic Play	• N/A

Notes: What did your child do well? Are there any skills they need to continue to work on?

B3. Building Shapes - Activity time: 20 minutes

Materials Needed:

☐ At least Four (4) pictures of animal homes without the animal ** Cut out pictures from Pet Store Ads or from pictures found online (example: dog crate, fish tank, reptile cage, chicken coop, hamster cage, etc.)
☐ One (1) Box of Crayons
☐ Two (2) Pieces of Blank Paper
☐ Four (4) 3x5 Index Cards (or the same number of index cards that there are pictures of animal homes.
☐ One (1) Yellow highlighter

Instructions:

Step 1: Sit with your child and show them the animal homes they cut out (from materials list).

Step 2: Ask your child what animal lives in each home.

Step 3: Write each animal the child says on one 3x5 index card. Write only one animal name per card. (*See Photo*)

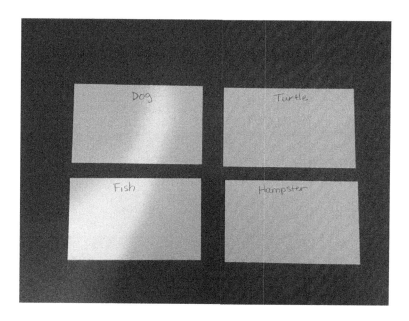

Step 4: Ask your child to trace the names of the animals on each 3x5 index card, with a yellow highlighter.

Step 5: Ask your child to use crayons to draw a picture of each animal that is on the 3x5 index card *(See Photo)*

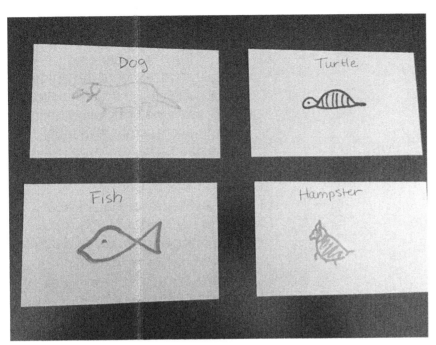

Step 6: On a Blank Piece of paper, Write the child's Name in a Vertical Line (See Example in Step 7).

Step 7: Once the child's name is written, help them sound out each letter of their name. Have them come up with a name for each of the animals they drew, using the letters of their name:

Example: **Sarah**

S ally
A manda
R yan
A dam
H enry

Step 8: Have your child assign one name from Step 7 to each animal in the 3x5 index card animal:

Example:

S ally   - Dog
A manda - Hampster
R yan - Fish
A dam - Turtle
H enry – Cat

Step 9: The adult should write each animal name (from Step 8) on the corresponding 3x5 index card (from Step 5).

Step 10: Ask your child to use a crayon trace to the name of each animal they chose.

B.3 Learning Objectives

Math/Science	Language/Literacy	Problem Solving	Motor Skills
• Classification • Matching	• Letter Identification • Emerging Writing • Name Identification • Phonetics	• Imagination and Creativity • Categorizing	• Fine Motor: Using Writing Utensils

Notes: What did your child do well? Are there any skills they need to continue to work on?

B4. HOME Hunt - Activity time: 20 minutes

Materials Needed:

☐ Eight (8) Sticky Notes
☐ One (1) One Pen
☐ One (1) Piece of Blank Paper

Instructions:

Step 1: Tell your child you're going to make a pattern with things that they find in their home.

Step 2: The adult should write down the following on a piece of paper:

> ## HOME
>
> TWO items that feel .... H ARD
> TWO items that can turn .... O FF
> TWO items that be used to ..... M EASURE
> TWO items that has............... E YES

Step 3: Ask your child to find items in your Home that match the descriptive words on the piece of paper in Step 2 (two items that are Hard, two items that can be turned Off, two items that can be used to Measure something and two items that have Eyes) – *See photo in Step 14*

Step 4: Have the child place all the items in the middle of the room.

Step 5: The adult should write the letter "H" on two sticky notes, the letter "O" on two sticky notes, the letter "M" on two sticky notes and the letter "E" on two sticky notes. – *See photo in Step 14*

Step 6: Ask your child to point to the two items are the ones that are **Hard**?

Step 7: The adult should put the sticky notes that have the letter "**H**" on those two "Hard" objects.

Step 8: Ask the child to point to the two items that can be turned **Off**?

Step 9: The adult should put the sticky notes that have the letter "**O**" on those two objects.

Step 10: Ask your child to point to the two items that can be used to **Measure** something?
Step 11: The adult should put the sticky notes that have the letter "**M**" on those two objects.

Step 12: Ask the child to point to the two items that have **Eyes**?

Step 13: The adult should put the sticky notes that have the letter "**E**" on those two objects.
Step 14: Next, place the items in a row to spell the letter "**H**" "**O**" "**M**" "**E**" with the sticky notes. See photo below:

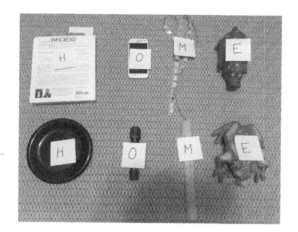

Step 15: Tell your child to create the following letter patterns by moving the objects with the corresponding letters (sticky note) on them. See photo examples below.

1. H.....E.....H.....E

2. M.....E.....M.....E
3. O.....H.....O.....H
4. O.....M.....E.....O.....M.....E

5. M.....O.....E.....M.....O.....E

Step 16: Are there other patterns the child can come up with?

B.4 Learning Objectives

Math/Science	Language/Literacy	Problem Solving	Motor Skills
• Number Identification • Utilizing Measuring Tools • Number Sense • Quantity and Counting	• Letter Identification • Emerging Writing • Word Identification • Phonetics	• Patterning • Categorizing • Understanding Functions of Items • Identifying Characteristics	• N/A

Notes: What did your child do well? Are there any skills they need to continue to work on?

B5. What Belongs Here? Rooms and their Things - Activity time: 20 minutes

Materials Needed:
- ☐ Five (5) Pieces of Blank White Paper
- ☐ One (1) Pen
- ☐ One (1) Yellow Highlighter
- ☐ One (1) Box of Crayons

Instructions:

Step 1: The adult should use a blue marker to write down the following words on blank pieces of paper. Write down one word on each piece of paper:

- Kitchen.
- Bathroom
- Bedroom
- Dining Room
- Living Room

Kitchen	Bathroom	Bedroom

Dining Room	Living Room

Step 2: The adult should show the child the paper with the word "Kitchen" written on it.

Step 3: Help the child sound out the word "Kitchen".

Step 4: Ask your child to use crayons to draw a picture of a kitchen and include items that are in the kitchen.

Step 5: Ask your child to identify objects that are in their pictures. The adult should use the pen to label these items.

Example:
Label – chair table, sink, cabinets, faucet, stove… anything your child describes.

Step 6: Repeat Steps 2 through 6 with the rest of the pieces of paper from Step 1.

Step 7: The adult should say: "There are lots of rooms in a home. In the home that You drew, there are five rooms. Each room has a lot of things in them. In the Kitchen, there are (read the labeled items listed on the pictures of the kitchen).

Step 8: Repeat step 7 for all of the pieces of paper from Step 5.

Take it to the next level:

Step 9: Ask your child to count how many items they labeled in each photo. The adult should write that number on the corresponding picture.

Step 10: Ask your child: "Which picture has the most items."

Step 11: Ask your child: "Which picture has the least items."

Step 12: Ask your child to identify each number written on the photos. Can they place the photos in order from least to most, based on the number written on the photo (from step 9)?

B.5 Learning Objectives

Math/Science	Language/Literacy	Problem Solving	Motor Skills
• Number Identification • Number Sense • Quantity and Counting • One to One Correspondence	• Letter Identification • Emerging Writing • Word Identification • Phonetics • New Vocabulary	• Categorizing • Identifying Characteristics	• Fine Motor: Using a Writing Tool

Notes: What did your child do well? Are there any skills they need to continue to work on?

Gross Motor – Using our large muscles to move

By Completing Level 2 Activities, We will learn...

- o **Uses gross motor movement skills to access a variety of obstacles and environments.**
- o **Hops on one foot, without support, three or more times.**
- o **Runs and Jumps over small objects.**

Fine Motor – Using our hands to complete tasks

By Completing Level 2 Activities, We will learn...

- o **Uses scissors appropriately.**
- o **Uses a crayon or pencil to draw or write.**

C1. Up on the Rooftop - Activity time: 15 minutes

☐ One (1) Wall
☐ One (1) Roll of Painters Tape
☐ One (1) Pen
☐ One (1) Tape Measure

Instructions:

Step 1: Tell the child they're going to pretend to be a home.

Step 2: Ask the child to stand with their back against a wall, feet flat on the floor and shoulders against the wall.

Step 3: The adult should put a 6-inch piece of painter's tape on the wall at the top of their child's head.

Tape

Step 4: Ask the child step away from the wall.

Step 5: The adult should use the tape measure to measure how many inches high the tape is from the ground.

Step 6: Use a pen to write the total inches on the painter's tape.

Step 7: Ask the child to stand with their back against a wall, feet flat on the floor with their arms straight up, reaching as far as they can towards the ceiling.

Make sure elbows are straight!

Step 8: The adult should put a 6-inch piece of painter's tape on the wall behind the child's hand.

Step 9: Ask the child step away from the wall.

Step 10: The adult should use the tape measure to measure how many inches are from the floor to the taped line from Step 8. Write the total inches on the painter's tape.

Step 11: Tell the child the first line (top of their head) from Step 3 is where the ceiling is in their pretend home.

Step 12: Tell the child the second line (top of their hand) from Step 8 is the top of their roof in their pretend home.

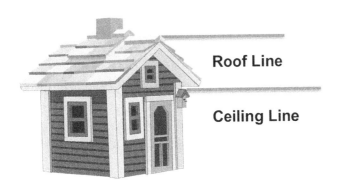

Roof Line

Ceiling Line

Step 13: Tell the child you are going to see if they can jump high enough to get "on the roof". Ask the child to put their hands straight above their head and jump as high as they can.

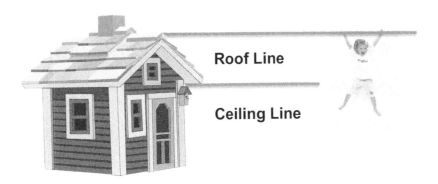

Roof Line

Ceiling Line

Step 14: Have the child face the wall and jump as high as they can. Can they touch a part of the wall that's higher than the "roof line" (the taped line from Step 8). Keep trying!

C.1 Learning Objectives

Math/Science	Language/Literacy	Problem Solving	Motor Skills
•Number Sense	•Following Directions •Using Size Words •Use Language in Conversation	•Understanding Measurement Concepts (Fast or Slow)	•Gross Motor: Jumping •Gross Motor: Body Awareness

Notes: What did your child do well? Are there any skills they need to continue to work on?

C2. Stairs or No Stairs - Activity time: 15 minutes

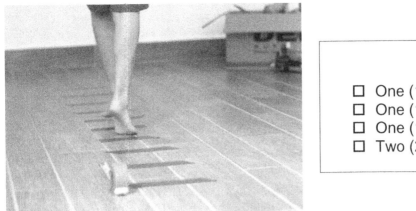

☐ One (1) Tape Measure
☐ One (1) Roll of Painter's Tape
☐ One (1) Marker
☐ Two (2) Pieces of Blank Paper

Instructions:

Step 1: The adult should cut 10 pieces of Painter's Tape. Each Piece should be at least 12 inches long.

Step 2: The adult should use a marker to write a large letter "B" on one piece of blank paper.

Step 3: The adult should use a marker to write a large letter "T" on the other piece of blank paper.

Step 4: The adult should place the piece of paper with a "B" on the floor. Place each 12-inch piece of painter's tape in a horizontal line, with four inches between each piece of tape (see visual below).

B | | | | | | | | | |
    4"   4"   4"   4"   4"   4"   4"   4"   4"

Step 5: Next place the piece of paper with the "T" on the floor at the end of the line.

B | | | | | | | | | | T
    4"   4"   4"   4"   4"   4"   4"   4"   4"

Step 6: Tell the child that the "B" represents the "Bottom" of the stairs. The "T" represents the "Top" of the stairs. **Each piece of tape represents one stair.**

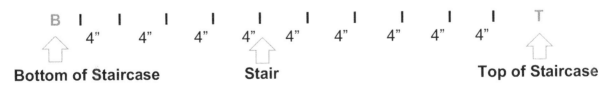

B | | | | | | | | | | T
    4"   4"   4"   4"   4"   4"   4"   4"   4"

Bottom of Staircase   **Stair**   **Top of Staircase**

Step 7: Tell the child to stand on the "Bottom" of the stairs (the paper that has the 'B" on it).

B | 4" | 4" | 4" | 4" | 4" | 4" | 4" | 4" | 4" T

Step 8: Now, ask the child to walk on each taped line (step), counting each line (step) they walk on (1 through 10). They will be done when they reach the "Top" of the stairs and stand on the letter "T".

Step 9: Great Job!!! Now tell the child you're going to increase the **"Width"** between each step to see if they can walk up the new "staircase".

Step 10: The adult should move each piece of tape 2 inches to the right, creating 6 inches between each piece of tape.

B | 6" | 6" | 6" | 6" | 6" | 6" | 6" | 6" | 6" T

Step 11: Repeat Step 9.

Step 12: Repeat Steps 10 and 11, **increasing the length between each of the "Stairs" by 2 inches** until the child can't reach the next "stair" while standing. How far can you increase the length to?

C.2 Learning Objectives

- Number Sense
- One to One Correspondence
- Counting to 10

- Following Directions
- Letter Identification

- Understanding Measurement Concepts (Fast or Slow)

- Gross Motor: Balance and Coordination

Notes: What did your child do well? Are there any skills they need to continue to work on?

C3. 1 Floor, 2 Floors, 3 Floors, More? - Activity time: 20 minutes

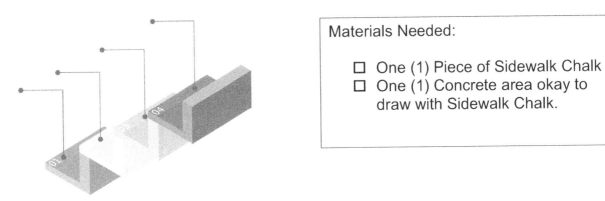

Materials Needed:

☐ One (1) Piece of Sidewalk Chalk
☐ One (1) Concrete area okay to draw with Sidewalk Chalk.

Instructions:

Step 1: Tell the child you're going to build a huge building that has 10 floors! That's a very tall building!

Step 2: The adult should use sidewalk chalk to draw a square that is large enough to fit the child's feet inside.

Step 3: The adult should use sidewalk chalk to write the number "1" inside the square.

Step 4: Tell the child to jump into the square. That square represents Floor number One "1" (the first floor). Ask the child to say **"One Floor".**

Step 5: Next, the adult should use sidewalk chalk to draw another square, above square "1" (See below):

Step 6: The adult should use sidewalk chalk to write the number "2" inside the new square.

Step 7: Tell the child to jump into Square 1 and Square 2 saying: "One plus One equals Two Floors".

Note: Encourage the child to add the "**s**" on the end of the word "floor" because more than one floor is plural.

Step 8: Next, the adult should use sidewalk chalk to draw another square above square "2".

Step 9: The adult should use sidewalk chalk to write the number "3" inside the new square.

Step 10: Tell the child to jump into Square 1, Square 2 and Square 3 saying:
> "**Two** plus One equals Three Floor**s**".

Note: Encourage the child to add the "**s**" on the end of floor.

Step 11: Repeat step 8 through 10 until there are Ten (10) floors/squares drawn.

Step 12: Have the child "Hop," on their right foot, through all of the squares saying: "There are Ten Floors".

Step 13: Repeat step 12 encouraging the child to "Hop" on their left foot.

C.3 Learning Objectives

Math/Science	Language/Literacy	Problem Solving	Motor Skills
•Number Sense/Identification •One to One Correspondence •Counting to 10 •Introduction to Addition	•Following Directions •Single vs Plural words	•Shape Identification	•Gross Motor: Jumping •Gross Motor: Hop on One Foot

Notes: What did your child do well? Are there any skills they need to continue to work on?

C4. Direction Maze - Activity time: 15 minutes

Materials Needed:
☐ One (1) Paper or Plastic Bag (Large)

Instructions:

Step 1: The adult should find two child-safe objects from each room in the house. Place each item into a paper or plastic bag.

Example:
- Kitchen: Spoon and Plastic Cup
- Bedroom: Pants and Pillow
- Play Room: 2 toys
- Bathroom: Toothpaste and Toilet Paper Roll

Step 2: Ask the child pull one object out of the bag.

Step 3: Ask the child "What room is this from?"

Step 4: Have the child jump all the way to the room the item is from. Ask them to put it away then return to you to see what else is in the bag.

Step 5: Repeat Step 2 through 4 until the child has placed all items back in their correct spot.

Step 6: The adult should find two more child-safe objects from each room in the home (repeat Step 1) and place them in the bag.

Step 7: Ask the child to pick one item from the bag.

Step 8: Ask the child "What room is that from?"

Step 9: Before the child puts that object away, ask them to pick out another item.

Step 10: Ask the child, "Where is that second item from?"

Take it to the Next Level:

Step 11: Tell the child to put the items back in the order they pulled them out! The item from step 7 should go back before the item from step 10.

Step 12: Can the child remember which item they pulled out first? The adult asks them to put the items away where they belong.

> **Example**: "Place the toothbrush on the sink in the bathroom and put the shoes in the floor in your closet."

C.4 Learning Objectives

Math/Science	Language/Literacy	Problem Solving	Motor Skills
•Number Sense/Identification	•Following Two-Step Directions •Vocabulary Building •Using Language in Conversation	•Recollection/Memory •Sorting •Categorizing •Organizing •Object Identification •Object Association	•Gross Motor: Jumping

Notes: What did your child do well? Are there any skills they need to continue to work on?

 **C5. Kitchen Jump** - Activity time: 20 minutes

Materials Needed:
- ☐ Four (4) Plastic Spoons
- ☐ Four (4) Plastic Forks
- ☐ Four (4) Plastic Knives

Instructions:

Step 1: Tell the child you're going to make patterns with the plastic utensils. This silverware is not to put in their mouths.

Step 2: The adult should lay the plastic utensils in the following pattern sequences. Make sure there is at least 6 inches between each piece of plastic ware:

- Plastic spoon, Plastic fork, Plastic spoon, Plastic fork, Plastic spoon, Plastic Fork

Step 3: Tell the child to jump over each piece of plastic utensils. While they are jumping, they need to name the piece of plastic ware they're jumping over:

Example: "spoon, fork, spoon, fork, spoon, fork."

Step 4: Now make a new pattern:

- Plastic knife, Plastic Fork, Plastic knife, Plastic Fork, Plastic knife, Plastic fork

Step 5: Repeat Step 3, asking the child to name the items they jump over.

Step 6: The adult should lay down the first four pieces of plastic ware in the following pattern, and see if the child can finish the pattern:

    <u>Adult</u>: Plastic Spoon, Plastic Knife, Plastic Spoon, Plastic Knife
    <u>Child</u>: Plastic Spoon, Plastic Knife

Step 7: Repeat Step 3, asking the child to name the items they jump over.

Step 8: The adult should lay down the first two pieces of plastic ware in the following pattern, and see if the child can finish the pattern:

    <u>Adult</u>: Plastic Fork, Plastic Spoon
    <u>Child</u>: Plastic Fork, Plastic Spoon, Plastic Fork, Plastic Spoon

Step 9: Repeat Step 3, asking the child name the items they jump over.

Take it to the Next Level:

Step 10: The adult should lay down the first three pieces of plastic-ware in the following **three-step pattern** and see if the child can finish the pattern:

Adult: Plastic Fork, Plastic Spoon, Plastic Knife
Child: Plastic Fork, Plastic Spoon, Plastic Knife, Plastic Fork, Plastic Spoon, Plastic Knife

Step 11: Repeat Step 3, requesting the child name the items they jump over.

Step 12: Repeat Step 10 and Step 11 with the following three-item patterns:

- Plastic Knife, Plastic Knife, Plastic Spoon
- Plastic Spoon, Plastic Fork, Plastic Knife
- Plastic Spoon, Plastic Spoon, Plastic Fork

Can the child come up with more patterns to complete?

C.5 Learning Objectives

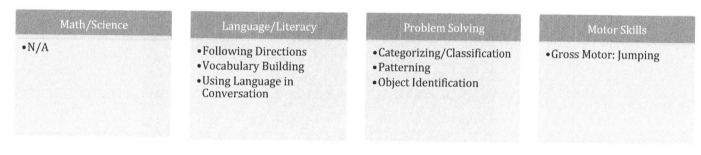

Math/Science	Language/Literacy	Problem Solving	Motor Skills
•N/A	•Following Directions •Vocabulary Building •Using Language in Conversation	•Categorizing/Classification •Patterning •Object Identification	•Gross Motor: Jumping

Notes: What did your child do well? Are there any skills they need to continue to work on?

Pre-K YOUR Way

Level 2 Unit 5

Space Exploration

Unit 5: Space

Themed Items For Indoor Learning Environment

Now that you have set up your environment, you are ready to place materials in it that directly relate to the theme you are studying! Here are some suggestions of materials your child can free-play with during the "Space" Theme:

Books: Age-appropriate books that directly correlate with the monthly theme can be found at your local library or bought separately online. This is a great opportunity to take a trip with your child to your local library and go on a search together. Have them identify words or pictures on the cover of children's books that correlate to the theme. Place a variety of books related to the theme in your child's book area. This will increase opportunities for them to expand their knowledge and use what they learn in the activities to comprehend what they read in the books.

Art Area: Encourage your child use this throughout each day by rotating items in an art area. These can be items have already been painted on, paper that they drew on already or leftover materials from another project. Thought provoking art projects are created when children are given unlimited opportunities to explore a variety of materials.

Some suggestions for the art area include:
- Crayons
- Paper
- Pens
- Empty Boxes (all kinds)
- Empty Toilet Paper or Paper Towel Rolls
- Foil
- Clean Q-tips for painting
- Scraps of paper
- Scraps of Yarn
- Scraps of any type of material – including fabric, sand paper, etc.
- Paper Bags
- Straws
- Popsicle Sticks
- Anything else that can be reused.

Sensory Bin Suggestions

A sensory bin is a small plastic bucket that is filled with a variety of materials. Sensory bins provide a space to engage in sensory-rich activities that offer opportunities to investigate textures while providing activities for relaxation and self-regulation. Sensory bins encourage language development, small motor development and control, spatial concepts, problem-solving skills and scientific observations. Each module includes a suggested sensory bin materials that correlate with the theme.

Set Up Instructions: In a Plastic Bucket, rotate the following sensory activities throughout the month.

- **Sand Writing Table:**
  Mix 2 cups of sand, 1 ½ cups cold water and 1 cup of cornstarch together. Stir the mixture for five to ten minutes over medium heat until it becomes thick. Pour the thick sand onto a cookie sheet. After it cools, have the child practice writing the Letter of the Week, writing the number of the week and drawing the Shape of the week on the sand.

  Note: You can also use this mixture to build sand castles that will stick together longer.

- **Planet Hunt:**
  Fill the plastic bucket up with black dirt. Count out eight "art pom-pom balls", Make sure that each pom-pom is a different color. Hide the pom-poms in the dirt. Allow the child to look for the pom-poms. When they find one, have them name one of the planets.

Dramatic Play Area

This play area allows children to understand and experience the adult world through imitation and creativity. The dramatic play area provides a safe space for young children to create stories while practicing new vocabulary and practicing social skills. It's also a space where groups of children engage in pretend play providing opportunities to learn self-help skills, share space and materials, take turns and the use abstract thinking. Each unite there is a list of suggested materials to integrate into this area, which correlates with the theme.

Suggested props to include in the Space dramatic play/pretend play area include:

- A child sized chair
- A Large Empty Box (could be a space ship, rocket, look-out spot, etc)
- Markers for Boxes
- Shoes
- Binoculars
- Star Stickers
- Balls (Planets)
- Black Construction Paper and White Chalk
- Telescope
- Pictures of Planets
- Pictures of Nature

Learning Objectives - Level 2

These activities have been developed to meet specific, age-appropriate, Kindergarten-Readiness skills. These skills are laid out in the learning objectives of each activity. The following activities may be completed in any order desired and are specifically designed to address the academic domains: math, science, language, literacy, cognitive, problem solving, and physical development. **After completing all modules in the Level 2 Curriculum Series, the child should be able to:**

Mathematics

- Identify objects by classification.
- Sort objects into categories by at least one attribute.
- Show understanding of measurement and begin to associate measurement descriptions (big, small, long, short).
- Recite numbers 1 through 10 in order.
- Count objects with one to one correspondence.
- Describe the similarities and differences of several shapes that include circle, triangle, square and rectangle.
- Create and finish simple patterns that include two elements.

Science/ Problem Solving Skills

- Develops solutions to a problem.
- Asks questions and performs simple investigations.
- Works through tasks that are difficult.
- Demonstrates understanding of visual and verbal prompts.

Language and Literacy

- Demonstrate the understanding that letters make words.
- Uses language to talk about past events.
- Uses words and increasing vocabulary to retell a story.
- Uses a variety of vocabulary to describe finding solutions to problems.
- Uses language in conversation to discover answers to questions.
- Name and match Uppercase letters.
- Accurately write all Letters of the Alphabet.
- Demonstrate Phonological Awareness of every Letter (The sounds that letters make).
- Follow simple two-step directions.

Gross Motor/Fine Motor Development

- Uses gross motor movement skills to access a variety of obstacles and environments.
- Hops on one foot, without support, three or more times.
- Runs and Jumps over small objects.
- Uses scissors appropriately.
- Uses a crayon or pencil to draw or write

Space Themed Academic Activities

These activities were developed to meet specific, age-appropriate, Kindergarten-Readiness skills. These skills are specified in the learning objectives of each activity. The following activities may be completed in any order desired and are specifically designed to address the academic domains: math, science, language, literacy, cognitive, problem solving, and physical development.

Each activity is on its own page. If the adult chooses to print out the activities, the space below each activity is provided for adults to write notes regarding the activity. Adults are encouraged to note if the child enjoyed the activity and if the child needs to work on specific learning objectives. Each activity can be repeated more than once to enable the child to master the learning objectives designed for that activity.

A. Math/Science Development
1. Planet Sun vs. Planet Moon
2. Distance Investigation
3. Planet Sizes
4. Pointing Stars
5. Space Travel

B. Language/Literacy Development
1. My Very Own Planet
2. Planet Alphabet
3. Who Lives Here?
4. Land vs. Water
5. Planet Names

C. Physical Development- Gross Motor & Fine-Motor
1. 3..2..1.. Blastoff
2. Planet Spin
3. Star Step
4. Space Walk
5. Dark and Light Pattern

Take it to the Next Level:
There are some activities which have a component included on how to "take an activity to the next level", increasing skill level related to the learning objectives laid out in that specific activity. Once the child has successful completed an activity, adults are encouraged to try the "take it to the next level" suggestions.

Mathematical Development – Understanding Numbers and their Purpose

By Completing Level 2 Activities, We will learn how to...

- o Identify objects by classification.
- o Sort objects into categories by at least one attribute.
- o Show understanding of measurement and begin to associate measurement descriptions (big, small, long, short).
- o Recite numbers 1 through 10 in order.
- o Count objects with one to one correspondence.
- o Describe the similarities and differences of several shapes that include circle, triangle, square and rectangle.
- o Create and finish simple patterns that include two elements.

Science/Cognitive Development – Learning How to Solve Problems

By Completing Level 2 Activities, We will learn how to..

- o Develop solutions to a problem.
- o Ask questions and performs simple investigations.
- o Work through tasks that are difficult.
- o Demonstrate understanding of visual and verbal prompts

A1. Planet Sun vs. Planet Moon - Activity time: 30 minutes

Materials Needed:
- ☐ One (1) Clock
- ☐ One (1) Timer
- ☐ One (1) Pen
- ☐ One (1) Piece of white chalk
- ☐ One (1) Piece of Blank White Paper
- ☐ One (1) Piece of Blank Black Construction Paper

Instructions:

- **Note: This activity should be started as soon as the child wakes up.**

Step 1: The adult should use the pen to write the word "**Day**" at the top of the white piece of paper.

Step 2: The adult should use a piece of white chalk to write the word "**Night**" on the black piece of construction paper.

Step 3: Tell your child they're going to find out how many hours of "sunlight" there are in their day and how many hours there are of "darkness" in their day.

Step 4: As soon as the child wakes up in the morning, have them look outside and tell the adult if it's **dark or light**.

Step 5: If it's dark, have them use the white piece of chalk to make a tally mark on the black piece of construction paper. If it's light, have them use the pen to make a tally mark on the white piece of paper.

Example:

Step 6: Use a phone, watch or portable timer to set the timer for **one hour.**

Step 7: Every hour, throughout the rest of the day, have the child look outside to see if it's light or dark and repeat Step 5, marking tallies on the paper.

Step 8: Before the child goes to bed, sit with them and count the total amount of tallies on the piece of white paper. Write that number on the paper. Tell the child that this number equals how many hours the sun was **up in the child's day.**

Step 9: Before the child goes to bed, sit down with them and count the total amount of tallies on the black construction paper. Write that number on the paper. Tell the child that this number equals how many hours the moon was **up in the child's day**.

Example:

A.1 Learning Objectives

Math/Science	Language	Problem Solving	Motor Skills
• Understanding Time • One to One Correspondence • Mathematical Operations • Number Identification	• Following New Directions	• Opposites • Categorization • Symbolic Representation (Colors)	• Fine Motor: Using a Writing Tool

Notes: What did your child do well? Are there any skills they need to continue to work on?

A2. Distance Investigation - Activity time: 15 minutes

Materials Needed:
- ☐ Two (2) Sheets of Blank, White Paper, cut into two Large Circles
- ☐ One (1) Package of 100 small star stickers or small circle garage sale stickers
- ☐ Ten (1)) Large 6" x 4" index cards
- ☐ One (1) Pen
- ☐ One (1) Box of Crayons

Instructions:

*Caution** – This may be a good opportunity to teach your child to never look directly at the sun because it can hurt their eyes.

Step 1: Have your child color one circle blue to represent plant earth.

Step 2: Have your child color one circle yellow to represent the sun.

Step 3: The adult should use a pen to write "Earth" on the Blue Circle and "Sun" on the Yellow circle.

Step 4: Ask your child to look out the window or door. Can they locate the sun? Ask them how far away they think the sun is from planet Earth.

Step 5: Tell them the sun in 93 million miles away from Planet Earth. That's a lot of miles!

> **Optional:** Take a ride in your car and tell your child when you have driven one mile. Ask them if that was far? The sun is 93 million miles away!

Step 6: The adult should write the number 10 on nine 6x4 index cards.

Step 7: The adults should write the number 3 on one 6x4 index card (not one that has a 10 on it).

Step 8: Ask your child to put the **same** amount of **stickers** as the number written on each index card.

> **Example:** Ten circle or star stickers put on the index cards that have the number 10 written on them. Three circle or star stickers on the i ndex card that has the number 3 written on it.

Step 9: The adult should place the Blue circle (planet Earth) on the floor.

Step 10: The adult should place the index cards in a horizontal line on the floor, starting with the blue circle ("earth"). **See Example Below:**

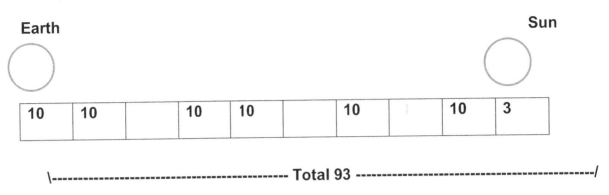

Step 11: The adult should place the _____ next to the last index card.

Step 12: Tell your child that each sticker represents 1 million miles! If they added up all the stickers on the index cards, it would equal **93 stickers**, representing **93 million miles** between planet Earth and the sun.

Take it to the next level:

Can your child jump 93 times?

A.2 Learning Objectives

Math/Science	Language	Problem Solving	Motor Skills
•One to One Correspondence •Mathematical Operations •Number Identification •Introduction to Addition •Introduction to Measurement	•Following New Directions •Develop Vocabulary •Letter and Word Identification	•Curiosity and Initiative •Categorization •Symbolic Representation (Colors) •Compare and Contrast	•Fine Motor: Placing Stickers/Developing Pincer Grasp •Gross Motor: Jumping

Notes: What did your child do well? Are there any skills they need to continue to work on?

A3. Planet Sizes - Activity time: 20 minutes

Materials Needed:
- ☐ Eight (8) Pieces of Blank Paper
- ☐ One (1) Black Marker
- ☐ One (1) Box of Crayons
- ☐ One (1) Pair of Adult Sized Scissors

Instructions:

Step 1: The adult should use scissors to cut eight circles out of a blank piece of paper. **Each circle a different size that can be organized from the smallest circle to the largest circle.**

Step 2: Ask your child to lay the circles, in a line, in the order of smallest to largest.

Step 3: Tell your child that you're going to find out which circles represent planets in the solar system.

Step 4: The adult should write the name of each Planet in the Corresponding Circle:

Plant List Smallest Circle to Largest Circle

Order (Small to Large)	Planet	Size (Diameter)
1 Smallest	**Mercury**	4,879.4 km
2	**Mars**	6,787 km
3	**Venus**	12,104 km
4	**Earth**	12,756 km
5	**Neptune**	49,528 km
6	**Uranus**	51,118 km
7	**Saturn**	120,660 km
8 Largest	**Jupiter**	142,800 km

Step 5: Read the names of the planets to your child. **Mercury is the smallest planet** (in size) and **Jupiter is the largest planet**.

Step 6: Allow your child to use crayons to decorate each planet.

Step 7: The adult should mix up all the circles and encourage the child to repeat Step 3.

A.3 Learning Objectives

Math/Science	Language	Problem Solving	Motor Skills
• One to One Correspondence • Number Identification • Introduction to Measurement • Understanding Size Concepts	• Following New Directions • Develop Vocabulary	• Curiosity and Initiative • Categorization • Symbolic Representation (Planet Size) • Compare and Contrast	• N/A

Notes: What did your child do well? Are there any skills they need to continue to work on?

A4. Pointing Stars - Activity time: 20 minutes

Materials Needed:

☐ One (1) Piece of Sidewalk Chalk
☐ A clear night where you can see stars

Instructions:

*Note: This activity will take place during the day and revisited at night.

Step 1: During the day, the adult should draw a picture of a 5-pointed star on the sidewalk with sidewalk chalk.

Step 2: Ask the child to count how many points are on the star (Answer: 5)

Step 3: Ask the child to write the number "5" on each point.

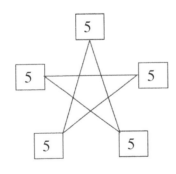

Step 4: Ask the child if they can find five objects that are the same.

Example: These children found 5 trains!

Step 5: Ask the child to draw another star with the sidewalk chalk **next to** the star the adult drew.

Step 6: That evening, take the child outside to where they can get a clear view of stars.

Step 7: Ask them if they can find five stars.

Step 8: Ask the child what the stars look like in the sky. Can they see the points on the ends?

A.4 Learning Objectives

Math/Science	Language	Problem Solving	Motor Skills
• One to One Correspondence • Number Identification • Quantity and Counting	• Following New Directions • Develop Vocabulary	• Curiosity and Initiative • Categorization • Investigation of Meaning	• Fine Motor: Using a Writing Tool (Chalk)

Notes: What did your child do well? Are there any skills they need to continue to work on?

A5. Space Travel- Activity time: 20 minutes

Materials Needed:
- ☐ Eight (8) Pieces of Paper
- ☐ One (1) Pen
- ☐ One (1) Box of Crayons

Instructions:

Step 1: Tell your child you're going to help them plan a trip to the moon.

Step 2: Tell them that they need to plan for **seven days**, which means the trip will take **one week.**

Step 3: The adult should use the pen to write one day of the week on each piece of paper.

Step 4: Lay the pieces of paper out in order, from Sunday through Saturday.

See Example Below:

Sunday	Monday	Tuesday	Wednesday	Thursday	Friday	Saturday

Step 5: Tell your child to think of items they might need for a one week vacation. First they're going to start with Sunday, the first day of the trip.

Step 6: The adult should ask the child what they do when they wake up. What would they need to bring with them for their morning? The adult should write the items down the child states on the paper that says "Sunday". **For Example:** toothbrush, towel and pajamas

Step 7: The adult should ask the child what he/she will wear for the day? The adult should write down the items the child states on the paper that says "Sunday". **For Example:** socks, shoes and a jacket.

Step 8: The adult should ask the child what they would eat? What will they need to bring with them for food? The adult should write the items down the child states on the paper that says "Sunday". **For Example:** cup, plate, water and a banana.

Step 9: Let's start looking at the rest of the week. The adult should then ask child what they would need for Monday? Will they still need clothes or food on Monday? Ask the child if they need to bring more than one toothbrush? Do they use a new one everyday, or do they just need to bring one they can reuse the rest of the week? Same with other items listed that day before, such as jackets and shoes.

Step 10: Repeat Steps 7 through 9 until they complete every day of the week.

Step 11: Ask your child to look at all of the items they have chosen to pack. Ask them to count the **total amount of items that are the same.** The adult should write the name of each item on a blank of paper and write the number of items next to them.

For Example:
- Banana's – 7
- Shirts – 7
- Toothpaste – 1 tube

Step 12: Tell your child to draw a picture of each item on the corresponding paper (Sunday through Saturday) that they need to pack.

Step 13: Tell them that you're going to pretend you really are going on the vacation. Can they find everything in their home they wrote down on their list?

Step 14: Allow the child to take the items to area and pretend to pack for the moon!

Step 15: Allow your child to take the items to an area and pretend they are going to the moon!

A.5 Learning Objectives

Math/Science	Language	Problem Solving	Motor Skills
• One to One Correspondence • Number Identification • Quantity and Counting • Understanding Time (Calendar)	• Following New Directions • Develop Vocabulary • Identifying Individual Needs	• Curiosity and Initiative • Categorization • Planning and Organization • Memory	• Fine Motor: Using a Writing Tool (Drawing)

Notes: What did your child do well? Are there any skills they need to continue to work on?

Language Development – Growing our Vocabulary

By Completing Level 2 Activities, We will learn how to…

- ○ Use language to talk about past events.
- ○ Use words and increasing vocabulary to retell a story.
- ○ Use a variety of vocabulary to describe finding solutions to problems.
- ○ Use language in conversation to discover answers to questions.
- ○ Follow simple two-step directions.

Literacy Development – Beginning Reading and Writing

By Completing Level 2 Activities, We will learn how to..

- ○ Demonstrate the understanding that letters make words.
- ○ Name and match Uppercase letters.
- ○ Accurately write all Letters of the Alphabet.
- ○ Demonstrate Phonological Awareness of every Letter (The sounds that letters make).

B1. My Very Own Planet - Activity time: 30 minutes

Materials Needed:
- ☐ Two (2) Pieces of Blank Paper
- ☐ One (1) Pen
- ☐ One (1) Box of Crayons or Markers

Instructions:

Step 1: Tell your child they're going to create a story about their very own planet.

Step 2: The adult should ask the following questions and write down your child's answers on a piece of blank paper:

- What types of objects are on your planet?
- How big is your planet?
- What is the weather like on the planet?
- Who lives on the planet?
- What types of food are on the plant?
- Where do people sleep on your planet?
- What do people do on your planet?
- What kinds of animals are on your planet?
- What is the name of your planet?

Step 3: Ask your child to tell you a story about something that happened on their planet.

Step 4: Encourage the child to use crayons or markers to draw a picture of their planet on a blank piece of paper.

B.1 Learning Objectives

Math/Science	Language/Literacy	Problem Solving	Motor Skills
• N/A	• Vocabulary building • Imagination and Creativity • Using Words to Form Ideas • Understanding the Letters make Words	• Imagination and Creativity • Answering Open-Ended Questions	• Fine Motor: Using Writing Tools

Notes: What did your child do well? Are there any skills they need to continue to work on?

B2. Planet Alphabet - Activity time: 15 minutes

Materials Needed:
- ☐ Twenty six (26) 3x5 cards (any color)
- ☐ One (1) Pen
- ☐ One (1) Marker (any color)

Instructions:

Step 1: Tell your child that our Solar System is a group of planets that **orbit** (move around) the sun.

Step 2: Tell your child they're going to create their own Solar System with the alphabet.

Step 3: The adult should write the letters **A through Z** (one letter each) on the 3x5 index cards.

Step 4: Tell your child they're going to help you come up with the name of each planet in their alphabet solar system. There are 26 letters in the alphabet, so the child will come up with 26 planet names, one for each letter.

Step 5: The adult should help the child sound out the letter of each alphabet and ask them to come up with a name for each letter. The adult should write down the name on the corresponding 3x5 index card.

Example:

R
Planet **R**obot

Step 6: Once the child has come up with a name for each letter (planet), place all of the 3x5 index cards on the table.

Step 7: Ask your child to trace the letter at the top of the 3x5 card with a black marker.

Step 8: Ask your child to identify and trace the same letter in the "planet name". In the example from Step 5, the child would trace the **"R"** on the top left corner of the 3x5 index card, and then trace the **"R"** in **R**obot.

Step 9: The adult should help the child place the index cards in **alphabetical order** (A-Z).

Step 10: The child should stand in one spot and place the 3x5 cards around them, on the floor, in the shape of a circle. The child symbolizes the **"sun"** and the circles will symbolize the **planets "orbiting"** around the sun.

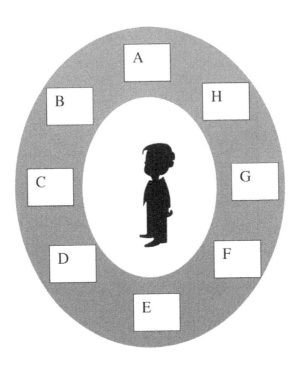

Take it to the next level:

Step 11: Tell your child that your child to jump on the letter that you call out. Start saying letters and see if your child can identify them by jumping to the card with the letter on it.

B.2 Learning Objectives

Math/Science	Language/Literacy	Problem Solving	Motor Skills
• Understands Cause and Effect (Planets Orbit)	• Vocabulary building • Letter Identification • Phonological Awareness • Understanding the Letters make Words	• Imagination and Creativity	• Fine Motor: Using Writing Tools

Notes: What did your child do well? Are there any skills they need to continue to work on?

B3. Who Lives Here - Activity time: 20 minutes

Materials Needed:
☐ Two (2) Sheets of Paper
☐ One (1) Pen

Instructions:

Step 1: Tell your child you're going to create a story about the **animals that live on planet Earth**. Tell the child that the adult is going to read a story, and it's their job to fill in the blanks.

Step 2: The adult should read the following story and use a pen to write down the words the child chooses to fill in the blanks with.

Story Title: Who Lives Here
A Story by: ___**(child's name)**___

This is a story about all the animals that live on my planet. My planet is called Planet

___**(name):**_____. On this planet, there are two animals that live

on the land. The first animal is called a ___**(name):**_____. They have

___**(how many):**_____ eyes, ___**(how many):**_____

nose/s and ___**(how many):**_____ ears. When they want to move

from one place to another they **(action word):**_____ with their feet. The

animal lives right next door to another animal that is much bigger. This animal is called a

(name):_____. He is ___**(how many):**_____ feet tall and

lives in a **(type of home):**_____. When these two animals

play together, they choose to play the game **(name of game):**_____.

One of my favorite things about this animal is that it **(what types of things does this animal do):** _____

_____ .

On my planet there are also **(name of animal):** _____ . They live in the water. These animals use their **(name a part of the body):** _____ to swim. When they want to breathe they **(action word):** _____ .

They eat a lot of things under water, but their favorite thing to eat is a **(name a food):** _____ .

These animals live **(how many):** _____ feet under the water. The only way to see them is to **(name an action word):** _____ .

The last group of animals that live on my planet live in the sky. They get around by

(name an action word): _____ . When they're tired and they want to sleep, they go to their beds that are in a **(place):** _____ .

Sometimes, when they're flying in the sky, they can see all of the animals on the land. One time they saw an animal **(name of the land animal from paragraph one):** _____ with another animal. It was really funny!

All of the animals on my planet are very special, whether they live on land, in the water or in the sky. The best part is they always laugh when **(name something they do):**

_____

_____

_____ .

The end.

Step 3: Re-read the story with all of the words/sentences filled in from what the child added.

Step 4: The adult should fold one piece of plank paper into three equal sections.

Step 5: The adult should use a pen to label one section "sky" another section "land" and the last section "water".

Water	Sky	Land

Step 6: Ask your child to draw a picture of each animal they talked about in their story. The animal that lives in the **sky** should be drawn on the part of the paper that says **"sky"**, the animal that lives on **land** should be drawn on the part of the paper that says **"land"** and the animal that lives in the **water** should be drawn on the part of the paper that says **"water"**.

Step 7: Once completed, ask the child to tell the adult a different story about the animals on the paper.

B.3 Learning Objectives

Math/Science	Language/Literacy	Problem Solving	Motor Skills
•Understands Cause and Effect (Planets Orbit) •Quantity and Counting	•Vocabulary Building •Letter Identification • Phonological Awareness •Understanding the Letters make Words •Completing a Story •Following Directions •Understanding Concepts of Print	•Imagination and Creativity •Answering Open-Ended Questions	•Fine Motor: Using Writing Tools

Notes: What did your child do well? Are there any skills they need to continue to work on?

B4. Land vs. Water - Activity time: 20 minutes

Materials Needed:

☐ Two (2) Pieces of Paper
☐ One (1) Pen
☐ One (1) Box of Crayons

Instructions:

Step 1: The adult should write the word **"Land"** on top of one piece of paper and the word **"Water"** on top of the other piece of paper.

Step 2: The adult should ask the following questions to the child about land and water. Write what the child says about "land" on the piece of paper that says "land" and write what the child says about "water" on the piece of paper that says "Water".

Questions to Ask	Land (Examples of Answers)	Water (Examples of Answers)
1. What does it feels like?	Dry	Wet
2. What does it looks like?	Brown	Blue
3. When people are on/in it they…	Walk	Swim
4. What do you where when you are in/on?	Shoes	Swim Suit
5. Do you drink it?	No	Yes
6. Are there trees on/in it?	Yes	Yes
7. Are there animals on/in it?	Yes	Yes
8. Can you drive on/in it?	Yes	No
9. Can you fly over it?	Yes	Yes
10. Can you play on/in it?	Yes	Yes

Step 3: There are lots of things that are different about land and water, but there are lots of things that are the same.

Step 4: Have the child use crayons to draw a picture of **"water"** on the back of the piece of paper that says **"water"**.

Step 5: Have the child use crayons to draw a picture of **"land"** on the back of the piece of paper that says **"land"**.

Take it to the next level:

Ask your child to use a pen or crayon to circle the answers that are the same for both land and water.

Example:

Questions to Ask	Land (Examples of Answers)	Water (Examples of Answers)
1. What does it feels like?	Dry	Wet
2. What does it looks like?	Brown	Blue
3. When people are on/in it they…	Walk	Swim
4. What do you where when you are in/on?	Shoes	Swim Suit
5. Do you drink it?	No	Yes
6. Are there trees on/in it?	Yes	Yes
7. Are there animals on/in it?	Yes	Yes
8. Can you drive on/in it?	Yes	No
9. Can you fly over it?	Yes	Yes
10. Can you play on/in it?	Yes	Yes

B.4 Learning Objectives

Math/Science	Language/Literacy	Problem Solving	Motor Skills
•Distinguishing Similar vs. Different	•Vocabulary Building • Completing a Story •Following Directions •Understanding Concepts of Print •Dictation •Using Words to Communicate	•Imagination and Creativity •Answering Open-Ended Questions	•Fine Motor: Using Writing Tools

Notes: What did your child do well? Are there any skills they need to continue to work on?

B5. Planets Names - Activity time: 20 minutes

Materials Needed:
- ☐ One (1) Piece of Blank Paper
- ☐ One (1) Pen
- ☐ One (1) Yellow Highlighter

Instructions:

Step 1: The adult should write a list of the names of the Planets in our Solar System on a blank piece of paper:

1. Mercury
2. Venus
3. Earth
4. Mars
5. Jupiter
6. Saturn
7. Uranus
8. Neptune

Step 2: Tell the child to count the letters in each planet name. Write the total next to each corresponding planet name.

Example:

1. Mercury ….. 8
2. Venus …. 5
3. Earth …. 5
4. Mars …. 4

Step 3: Tell your child to use a blue crayon to circle all of the M's they see when looking at all of the Planet names.

Example: Circle the M in Mercury and the M in Mars.

Step 4: Tell the child to use a green crayon to circle all of the V's they see in the list of names starting with the "V" for Venus.

Step 5: Tell the child to use a red crayon to circle all of the E's they see in the list of names starting with the "E" for Earth.

Step 6: Tell the child to use a ⟶ to circle all of the **J's** they see in the list of names starting with the "J" for **Jupiter**.

Step 7: Tell the child to use a **Purple crayon** to circle all of the **S's** they see in the list of names starting with the "**S**" for **S**aturn.

Step 8: Tell the child to use a Pink crayon to circle all of the U's they see in the list of names starting with the "U" for Uranus.

Step 9: Tell the child to use an Orange crayon to circle all of the N's they see in the list of names starting with the "N" for Neptune.

Example:

1. Mercury
2. Venus
3. Earth
4. Mars
5. Jupiter
6. Saturn
7. Uranus
8. Neptune

Step 10: Ask the child to count how many letters are circled with each color and write each total using the same color crayon.

Example: M 2   E 6   U 6

Step 11: When completed, ask the child if there are any numbers that are the same. What letters have the same amount of numbers (For Example: there are **6 E's** and **6 U's.**

Step 12: Ask the child what letter do they see the **most of**? Which letter do they see **the least of?**

B.4 Learning Objectives

Math/Science	Language/Literacy	Problem Solving	Motor Skills
• Distinguishing Similar vs. Different • Quantity and Counting • One to One Correspondence	• Vocabulary Building • Letter and Word Knowledge • Letter Identification • Introduction to Spelling and Letters make Words	• Identifying Colors	• Fine Motor: Using Writing Tools

Notes: What did your child do well? Are there any skills they need to continue to work on?

Gross Motor – Using our large muscles to move

By Completing Level 2 Activities, We will learn...

- o **Uses gross motor movement skills to access a variety of obstacles and environments.**
- o **Hops on one foot, without support, three or more times.**
- o **Runs and Jumps over small objects.**

Fine Motor – Using our hands to complete tasks

By Completing Level 2 Activities, We will learn...

- o **Uses scissors appropriately.**
- o **Uses a crayon or pencil to draw or write.**

C1. 3...2...1...Blastoff - Activity time: 30 minutes

Materials Needed:
- ☐ One (1) Roll of Painter's Tape
- ☐ One (1) area to run!

Instructions:

Step 1: The adult should place five 16-inch pieces of painter's tape around the room.

Step 2: Tell the child that you're going to say the words "3, 2, 1 then Blastoff". Here are the rules to the game:

- When the adult says **3,** the child should **tap their nose three times**.

- When the adult says **2,** the child should **clap their hands two times.**

- When the adult says **1,** the child should **jump one time.**

- When the adult says "**Blastoff**" the child should **run around the room.** When the child comes across a line of **painter's tape, they must jump over it!**

Step 3: After the child jumps over all of the tape, then the game starts over with the adult stating "3, 2, 1, Blastoff". Repeat as many times as you would like!

C.1 Learning Objectives

Math/Science	Language/Literacy	Problem Solving	Motor Skills
•Number Sense •Counting Backwards	•Following Directions	•Association	•Gross Motor: Jumping •Gross Motor: Body Awareness •Gross Motor: Coordination •Gross Motor: Beginning Obstacle Course Challenge •Fine Motor: Eye-Hand Coordination

Notes: What did your child do well? Are there any skills they need to continue to work on?

C2. Planet Spin - Activity time: 15 minutes

Materials Needed:
- ☐ One (1) Yellow Object
- ☐ One (1) Piece of Sidewalk Chalk
- ☐ Five (5) Popsicle Sticks
- ☐ One (1) Empty Container

Instructions:

Step 1: Have the child find an object that is Yellow that can be easily moved and not breakable.

Step 2: Place the yellow object in the middle of a floor.

Step 3: The adult should use sidewalk chalk to draw a large circle around the yellow object.

Step 4: Tell the child the yellow object is the "sun".

Step 5: Tell the child they're going to be a planet orbiting around the "sun".

Step 6: The adult should write the numbers 1 through 5 on popsicle sticks, one number should be written on each popsicle stick. Place the popsicle sticks into an empty container.

Step 7: Tell the child to stand on the **circle** that is around the **"sun"** (**yellow** object).

Step 8: Tell the child that when planets orbit around the sun they spin slowly.

Step 9: The adult should pick a popsicle stick.

Step 10: Show the popsicle stick to the child and ask them to name the number.

Step 11: Have the child walk on the chalk line, while slowly spinning, the same number of times that is written on the popsicle stick.

For Example: If the popsicle stick has the number 5 written on it, then the child should spin around in a circle 5 times while trying to walk on the chalk line.

Step 12: Repeat Steps 9 through 11 until the child has completed **one orbit around the "sun"** (when they have spun in circles on the chalk line and reached the spot they started in Step 7)

** **Important** – It is important for the child to take frequent breaks during this activity so they don't get dizzy.

C.2 Learning Objectives

Math/Science	Language/Literacy	Problem Solving	Motor Skills
• Number Sense • One to One Correspondence • Number Identification • Understanding Scientific Concepts	• Following Directions	• Shape Identification	• Gross Motor: Body Awareness • Gross Motor: Coordination • Gross Motor: Balance

Notes: What did your child do well? Are there any skills they need to continue to work on?

C3. Star Step - Activity time: 20 minutes

Materials Needed:
- ☐ Six (6) Popsicle sticks
- ☐ One (1) Piece of Sidewalk Chalk
- ☐ Two (2) Empty Containers

Instructions:

Step 1: The adult should write one Blue number "5" on the bottom half of two popsicle sticks.

Step 2: The adult should write one Red number "5" on the bottom half of two popsicle sticks.

Step 3: The adult should write one Green number "5" on the bottom half of two popsicle sticks.

Step 4: The adult should use sidewalk chalk to write a 6 -foot-tall **"S"** on the sidewalk.

Step 5: The adult should put one popsicle stick with a green "5", one popsicle stick with a blue "5" and one popsicle stick with a red "5" in an empty container **with the "5's " facing down.**

Step 6: The adult should put the other popsicle sticks with a green "5", blue "5" and red "5" in the other empty container, **with the "5's" facing down.**

Step 7: Tell the child that the **"S"** made with the chalk stands for the word **"star".** Have the child stand at one end of the **"S".**

Step 8: Tell the child to pick one popsicle stick out of each container.

Step 9: If the popsicle sticks match (the same color **5's** on both) then the child can take 5 steps along the "S" line. Make sure they count each step out loud. Tell them that they are taking **5 steps** because there are **5 points on a star.**

Step 10: If the popsicle sticks **do not match,** the child must **pick two more** until they find two that do match.

Step 11: Place the popsicle sticks back into their original containers.

Step 12: Repeat Step 8 through Step 10 until the child walks all the way to the opposite end of the **"S".**

C.3 Learning Objectives

Math/Science	Language/Literacy	Problem Solving	Motor Skills
• Number Sense: Quantity and Counting • One to One Correspondence • Number Identification	• Following Directions • Letter Identification	• Shape Identification • Matching • Identifying Colors	• Gross Motor: Body Awareness • Gross Motor: Coordination • Gross Motor: Balance

Notes: What did your child do well? Are there any skills they need to continue to work on?

C4. Space Walk - Activity time: 20 minutes

Materials Needed:
- ☐ One (1) Stick of Sidewalk Chalk
- ☐ Eight (8) 3x5 cards, any color
- ☐ One (1) Ruler

Instructions:

Step 1: The adult should write the following letters on the 3x5 index cards. Write only one letter per card:

1. M
2. V
3. E
4. J
5. S
6. U
7. N

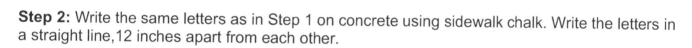

Step 2: Write the same letters as in Step 1 on concrete using sidewalk chalk. Write the letters in a straight line, 12 inches apart from each other.

Step 3: Tell the child that **each of the letters** is the **first letter of all the planets in our solar system:**

1. **M**ars and **M**ercury
2. **V**enus
3. **E**arth
4. **J**upiter
5. **S**aturn
6. **U**ranus
7. **N**eptune

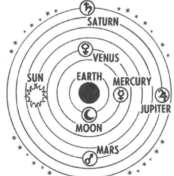

Step 4: Tell your child that you are going to play a game. They're going to pretend they are in space and jump from planet to planet. **In space, there is no gravity, so when they move from one planet to the next, they need to jump.** Since there is no gravity in space, people float in the air instead of walking on the ground.

Step 5: Show the child one of the 3x5 index cards and ask them to **name the letter**. Once identified, have the child look for that letter on the ground, written in chalk, and stand on it.

Step 6: The adult should pick another 3x5 index card. Have the child **name that letter**. Once identified, the child should jump to that same letter, written in chalk, on the ground. Remind them that they can only take a break when they're on a letter because **there is no gravity when they are not on a planet.**

Step 7: Repeat Step 7 until all letters have been "jumped" to.

Step 8: Continue playing as long as you like.

C.4 Learning Objectives

Math/Science	Language/Literacy	Problem Solving	Motor Skills
• Understanding Scientific Terms	• Following Directions • Letter Identification	• Creativity and Imagination	• Gross Motor: Body Awareness • Gross Motor: Coordination • Gross Motor: Jumping

Notes: What did your child do well? Are there any skills they need to continue to work on?

C5. Dark and Light Pattern - Activity time: 20 minutes

Materials Needed:
- ☐ One (1) Piece of paper
- ☐ One (1) Box of Crayons
- ☐ One (1) Pen

Instructions:

Step 1: The adult should tell the child they're going to make patterns with some items. They are going to use things that are outside during the day and some others that can only be seen at night.

Step 2: Ask your child to name things they see in the sky when it's light outside.

Step 3: Ask your child to name things they see in the sky when it is dark outside.

Step 4: The adult should gather a **yellow crayon**, a blue crayon and an orange crayon.

Step 4: The adult should draw the following patterns on the blank piece of paper. Use the following color and word key to know which color crayon to use:

What do draw	What it represents
A Yellow Circle	The Sun
A Blue Half-Circle	The Moon
An Orange Star	One Star

Patterns to draw:

1. Sun, Sun, Moon, Sun, Sun, Moon

2. Sun, Moon, Moon, Sun, Moon, Moon

3. Sun, Star, Moon, Sun, Star, Moon

4. Moon, Sun, Star, Moon, Sun Star

5. Star, Star, Moon, Star, Star Moon

Step 5: Once the adult has drawn the patterns from Step 4, ask your child to continue the patterns using the **same colors and shapes** as the parent. The child can either draw the pattern on the same page as the adult or they can use a new piece of paper.

C.5 Learning Objectives

Math/Science	Language/Literacy	Problem Solving	Motor Skills
• N/A	• Following Directions • Building Vocabulary	• Patterns • Classification • Visual Representation	• Fine Motor: Drawing with Crayons

Notes: What did your child do well? Are there any skills they need to continue to work on?

Pre-K YOUR Way

Level 2 Unit 6

Advanced Numbers, Colors and Shapes

Unit 6: Advanced Numbers, Letters and Shapes

Now that you have set up your environment, you are ready to place materials in it that directly relate to the theme you are studying! Here are some suggestions of materials your child can free-play with during the "Advanced Numbers, Letters and Shapes" Theme:

Books: Age-appropriate books that directly correlate with the monthly theme can be found at your local library or bought separately online. This is a great opportunity to take a trip with your child to your local library and go on a search together. Have them identify words or pictures on the cover of children's books that correlate to the theme. Place a variety of books related to the theme in your child's book area. This will increase opportunities for them to expand their knowledge and use what they learn in the activities to comprehend what they read in the books.

Art Area: Encourage your child use this throughout each day by rotating items in an art area. These can be items have already been painted on, paper that they drew on already or leftover materials from another project. Thought provoking art projects are created when children are given unlimited opportunities to explore a variety of materials.

Some suggestions for the art area include:
- Crayons
- Paper
- Pens
- Empty Boxes (all kinds)
- Empty Toilet Paper or Paper Towel Rolls
- Foil
- Clean Q-tips for painting
- Scraps of paper
- Scraps of Yarn
- Scraps of any type of material – including fabric, sand paper, etc.
- Paper Bags
- Straws
- Popsicle Sticks
- Anything else that can be reused.

Sensory Bin Suggestions

A sensory bin is a small plastic bucket that is filled with a variety of materials. Sensory bins provide a space to engage in sensory-rich activities that offer opportunities to investigate textures while providing activities for relaxation and self-regulation. Sensory bins encourage language development, small motor development and control, spatial concepts, problem-solving skills and scientific observations. Each module includes a suggested sensory bin materials that correlate with the theme.

Set Up Instructions: In a Plastic Bucket, rotate the following sensory activities throughout the month.

- **Sand Writing Table:**
  Mix 2 cups of sand, 1 ½ cups cold water and 1 cup of cornstarch together. Stir the mixture for five to ten minutes over medium heat until it becomes thick. Pour the thick sand onto a cookie sheet. After it cools, have the child practice writing the Letter of the Week, writing the number of the week and drawing the Shape of the week on the sand.

  Note: You can also use this mixture to build sand castles that will stick together longer.

- **Sensory Patterns:**
  Place two gallons of sand in a sensory bin. Add a variety of materials that are able to to be sorted by shape, colors, size or texture into the sensory bin. Some examples include the following:
  a. Animals that can be patterned by color
  b. Animals that can be patterned by big vs. small
  c. Blocks of a variety of shapes, colors and sizes that can form a pattern.
  d. Different sizes and colors of plastic toys that can be formed into a pattern (plastic cars)

Dramatic Play Area

This play area allows children to understand and experience the adult world through imitation and creativity. The dramatic play area provides a safe space for young children to create stories while practicing new vocabulary and practicing social skills. It's also a space where groups of children engage in pretend play providing opportunities to learn self-help skills, share space and materials, take turns and the use abstract thinking. Each unite there is a list of suggested materials to integrate into this area, which correlates with the theme.

Suggested props to include in the Space dramatic play/pretend play area include:

- Letter Cards
- Empty Boxes
- Blocks of all shapes and sizes
- Any objects that have shapes, letters or numbers on them
- Blocks or manipulative that have multiple colors for patterning

Learning Objectives - Level 2

These activities have been developed to meet specific, age-appropriate, Kindergarten-Readiness skills. These skills are laid out in the learning objectives of each activity. The following activities may be completed in any order desired and are specifically designed to address the academic domains: math, science, language, literacy, cognitive, problem solving, and physical development. **After completing all modules in the Level 2 Curriculum Series, the child should be able to:**

Mathematics

- Identify objects by classification.
- Sort objects into categories by at least one attribute.
- Show understanding of measurement and begin to associate measurement descriptions (big, small, long, short).
- Recite numbers 1 through 10 in order.
- Count objects with one to one correspondence.
- Describe the similarities and differences of several shapes that include circle, triangle, square and rectangle.
- Create and finish simple patterns that include two elements.

Science/ Problem Solving Skills

- Develops solutions to a problem.
- Asks questions and performs simple investigations.
- Works through tasks that are difficult.
- Demonstrates understanding of visual and verbal prompts.

Language and Literacy

- Demonstrate the understanding that letters make words.
- Uses language to talk about past events.
- Uses words and increasing vocabulary to retell a story.
- Uses a variety of vocabulary to describe finding solutions to problems.
- Uses language in conversation to discover answers to questions.
- Name and match Uppercase letters.
- Accurately write all Letters of the Alphabet.
- Demonstrate Phonological Awareness of every Letter (The sounds that letters make).
- Follow simple two-step directions.

Gross Motor/Fine Motor Development

- Uses gross motor movement skills to access a variety of obstacles and environments.
- Hops on one foot, without support, three or more times.
- Runs and Jumps over small objects.
- Uses scissors appropriately.
- Uses a crayon or pencil to draw or write

Part 1: Advanced Numbers, Colors and Shapes - Academic Activities

These activities were developed to meet specific, age-appropriate, Kindergarten-Readiness skills. These skills are specified in the learning objectives of each activity. The following activities may be completed in any order desired and are specifically designed to address the academic domains: math, science, language, literacy, cognitive, problem solving, and physical development.

Each activity is on its own page. If the adult chooses to print out the activities, the space below each activity is provided for adults to write notes regarding the activity. Adults are encouraged to note if the child enjoyed the activity and if the child needs to work on specific learning objectives. Each activity can be repeated more than once to enable the child to master the learning objectives designed for that activity.

A. Math/Science Development
1. Colorful Fish
2. Boat Races
3. Sea Salt Shapes
4. Underwater Life
5. Number Shape or Color Sort

B. Language/Literacy Development
1. Spelling My Name in Water
2. Spelling Numbers
3. One to One Popsicle
4. Shapley Letters
5. Body Numbers

C. Physical Development - Gross Motor & Fine-Motor
1. Side Shape Count
2. Patterned Numbers
3. Measurement Spoons
4. Scissor Snip
5. Number and Color Scramble

Take it to the Next Level:
There are some activities which have a component included on how to "take an activity to the next level", increasing skill level related to the learning objectives laid out in that specific activity. Once the child has successful completed an activity, adults are encouraged to try the "take it to the next level" suggestions.

Mathematical Development – Understanding Numbers and their Purpose

By Completing Level 2 Activities, We will learn how to...

- o Identify objects by classification.
- o Sort objects into categories by at least one attribute.
- o Show understanding of measurement and begin to associate measurement descriptions (big, small, long, short).
- o Recite numbers 1 through 10 in order.
- o Count objects with one to one correspondence.
- o Describe the similarities and differences of several shapes that include circle, triangle, square and rectangle.
- o Create and finish simple patterns that include two elements.

Science/Cognitive Development – Learning How to Solve Problems

By Completing Level 2 Activities, We will learn how to..

- o Develop solutions to a problem.
- o Ask questions and performs simple investigations.
- o Work through tasks that are difficult.
- o Demonstrate understanding of visual and verbal prompts

A1. Colorful Fish - Activity time: 30 minutes

Materials Needed
- ☐ Red, Blue, Green and Yellow Finger paint
- ☐ Four (4) small bowls or paper cups
- ☐ Four (4) small paintbrushes
- ☐ Four (4) pieces of paper cut into the shape of fish

Instructions:

Step 1: The adult should place three tablespoons of each finger paint color in their own bowl or paper cup. Place one small paintbrush into each bowl/cup.

Step 2: Put one paper fish on the table and ask the child to paint the fish red and blue. What happens when you mix the two colors together? (Answer: **Purple**)

Step 3: Put one paper fish on the table and ask the child to paint the fish red and green. What happens when you mix the two colors together? (Answer: Brown)

Step 4: Put one paper fish on the table and ask the child to paint the fish   and blue. What happens when you mix the two colors together? (Answer: Green)

Step 5: Put one paper fish on the table and ask the child to paint the fish red and   . What happens when you mix the two colors together? (Answer: Orange)

Step 6: Tell the child that **four of the colors in the cups are called primary colors**. When primary colors are mixed together, they make new colors.

Step 7: Place the painted fish up to dry.

A.1 Learning Objectives

Math/Science	Language	Problem Solving	Motor Skills
• Color Qualities	• Following Directions • Using Descriptive Words • Answering Open-Ended Questions	• Color Identification • Primary Colors • Cause and Effect	• Fine Motor: Advanced Writing grasp

Notes: What did your child do well? Are there any skills they need to continue to work on?

A2. Boat Races - Activity time: 30 minutes

Materials Needed
- ☐ Orange Peel
- ☐ One (1) Stick
- ☐ One (1) Empty water bottle
- ☐ Bathtub
- ☐ Water
- ☐ One (1) Kitchen Scale

Instructions:

*** **Caution:** Children should never be left unattended around standing water.

Step 1: The adult should fill the bathtub with one inch of water.

Step 2: Place the orange peel, the stick and the empty water bottle into the water.

Step 3: Ask the child: "Do the items sink or float?"

Step 4: Have the child blow on one side of each item and see which one is easier to move with their "wind" (their breath). Ask them:
- "Which one moves the fastest? Why?"
- "Which one moves the slowest? Why?"

Step 5: Take each item out of the water and place them next to the scale.

Step 6: Help the child place each item individually on a kitchen scale. The adult should write down the numbers that each one weighs on a piece of paper.

Step 7: Ask the child the following questions:
- "Which one is the heaviest? Is that the one that moved the slowest?"
- "Which is the lightest? Is that the one that moved the quickest?"

Step 8: Ask the child to look at the numbers (the weight of each item) and answer these questions:
- "Which number is larger? Why?"
- "Which item is the smaller? Why?"

Take it to the Next Level:
1) Find other items around the house and repeat the activity.
2) Ask the child: "what qualities of each item make it either sink or float?"
3) Can the child decide if one is heavier than the other item?
4) Encourage the child to weigh each product on the scale and see if the heavier object sinks and the lighter object floats.

A.2 Learning Objectives

Math/Science	Language	Problem Solving	Motor Skills
• Number Sense • Number Identification • Curiosity and Initiative • Understanding Number Concepts • Understanding Weight	• Following Directions • Using Descriptive Words • Answering Open-Ended Questions • Vocabulary Development	• Classification • Cause and Effect	• N/A

Notes: What did your child do well? Are there any skills they need to continue to work on?

A3. Sea Salt Shapes   Activity time: 30 minutes

Materials Needed
☐ One (1) bottle of Elmer's Gl[
☐ One-quarter (¼) cup Sand
☐ One-quarter (¼) cup Salt
☐ One (1) Piece of Paper
☐ One (1) box of Markers
☐ One (1) Small Paintbrush

Instructions:

Step 1: On a blank piece of paper, the adult should draw:
- one **small** triangle
- one **large** triangle
- one **small** square
- one **large** square
- one **small** circle
- one **large** circle
- one **small** rectangle
- one **large** rectangle

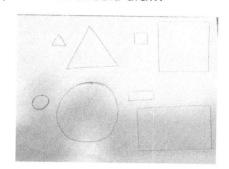

Step 2: Place 1/8 cup of Elmer's Glue in a paper cup.

Step 3: Ask the child to find the "**small triangle**". Have them put glue on **one** side, **then add some salt.**

Step 4: Ask the child to identify the rest of the **small** shapes and paint them with the **salt.**

Step 5: Ask the child to find the "**large rectangle**". Once they find it, have them put glue on **one** side of it and **add some sand.**

Step 6: Ask the child to identify the rest of the **large** shapes and paint them with **sand**.

Step 7: Ask the child the following questions:
- How many triangles are there?
- How many circles are there?
- How many squares are there?
- How many rectangles are there?
- How many small shapes are there?
- How many large shapes are there?

Step 10: Allow the child to place the shapes into the dramatic play/pretend play area, adding the shapes to different creations. Can they label each object by shape and size in a new play space?

A.3 Learning Objectives

Math/Science	Language	Problem Solving	Motor Skills
• Shape Identification • Size Identification • One to One Correspondence • Sensory Activities	• Following Directions • Using Descriptive Words • Answering Open-Ended Questions • Vocabulary Development	• Classification • Sorting • Categorizing • Understanding Opposites	• Fine Motor: Gluing • Fine Motor: Grasp

Notes: What did your child do well? Are there any skills they need to continue to work on?

A4. More vs. Less - Activity time: 20 minutes

Materials Needed
- ☐ Three (3) to Four (4) Couch Cushions/Pillows
- ☐ One (1) or Two (2) Blankets
- ☐ One (1) Flashlight
- ☐ Books
- ☐ One (1) Blank Piece of Paper
- ☐ One (1) Set of Markers or Crayons

Instructions:

Step 1: Show your child some pictures of tents. You can do this by going to look at the camping area in a local store, looking at an outdoor magazine or looking at an Internet site (such as campingworld.com). You can also look for tent photos on the Internet.

Step 2: Ask your child to identify different parts of the tent. Include the following questions:
- Where are the doors?
- Where are the windows
- Is there a roof?
- Is there a floor?

Step 3: Show your child the couch cushions, pillows and blankets.

Step 4: Ask them to use the crayons/markers and paper draw a picture of how he/she will make a tent with the materials listed in Step 3.

Step 5: After your child has drawn their photos, tell them that this picture is called a plan/diagram. Can they identify all of the tent parts discussed in Step 2?

Step 6: Ask the child to use their diagram (photo from Step 4) to answer the following questions about their tent. Have them write down the number they say next to the item on their diagram:

- How many doors are there in your tent?
- How many windows are there in your tent ?
- How many pillows should we put in the tent?
- How many sleeping bags should we put in the tent?

Step 6: Assist the child in building the tent they drew in the plan, using the materials from the materials list in this activity.

Step 7: When completed, look at the plan. Is the door in the same place as drawn on their plan? Are the other parts of the tent in the same places they are on the diagram?

Step 8: Once the tent is complete, place some books and a flashlight inside of the tent and allow the child to read in it!

A.4 Learning Objectives

Math/Science	Language	Problem Solving	Motor Skills
• One to One Correspondence • Quantity and Counting • Introduction to Plan and Development	• Following Directions • Using Descriptive Words • Answering Open-Ended Questions • Vocabulary Development	• Classification • Categorizing • Imagination and Creativity • Cause and Effect	• Fine Motor: Using a Writing Tool • Gross Motor: Moving large objects

Notes: What did your child do well? Are there any skills they need to continue to work on?

A5. Number/Color Sort - Activity time: 20 minutes

Materials Needed
- ☐ Five (5) Objects that are green
- ☐ Four (4) Objects that are red
- ☐ Three (3) Objects that are blue
- ☐ Two (2) Objects that are black
- ☐ One (1) Object that is white

Instructions:

Step 1: Tell the child you're going to use a variety of objects to sort and count.

Step 2: Encourage the child to count how many green objects there are (Answer: 5).

Step 3: Encourage the child to count how many red objects there are (Answer 4).

Step 4: Encourage the child to count how many blue objects there are (Answer 3).

Step 5: Encourage the child to count how many **black objects** there are (Answer 2).

Step 6: Encourage the child to count how many white objects there are (Answer 1).

Step 7: Now ask the child to count the **total amount of all of the objects** (Answer 15). They can find this answer by counting all of the objects. They do not need to add numbers together!

Step 8: Ask the child to pick out **six objects** – 3 objects of one color and 3 objects of another.

Step 9: Ask them to create a simple two-color pattern using the ten objects?

　　　Example: blue, green, blue, green

Step 10: Ask the child to choose **ten new objects** from the pile (any color).

Step 11: Repeat Step 9. How many different patterns can they make out of those 10 objects?

Step 12: Repeat step 10 and 11 five times.

Take it to the Next Level:

Can the child create a **three-color pattern**? Examples include:
- Green, Blue, Red, Green, Blue, Red
- Green, **Black**, Blue, Green, **Black**, Blue

A.5 Learning Objectives

Math/Science	Language	Problem Solving	Motor Skills
• One to One Correspondence • Recite 1 through 10 in Order • Quantity and Counting	• Following Directions • Using Descriptive Words • Vocabulary Development	• Classification • Categorizing • Patterning • Color Identification	• N/A

Notes: What did your child do well? Are there any skills they need to continue to work on?

.

Language Development – Growing our Vocabulary

By Completing Level 2 Activities, We will learn how to…

- Use language to talk about past events.
- Use words and increasing vocabulary to retell a story.
- Use a variety of vocabulary to describe finding solutions to problems.
- Use language in conversation to discover answers to questions.
- Follow simple two-step directions.

Literacy Development – Beginning Reading and Writing

By Completing Level 2 Activities, We will learn how to..

- Demonstrate the understanding that letters make words.
- Name and match Uppercase letters.
- Accurately write all Letters of the Alphabet.
- Demonstrate Phonological Awareness of every Letter (The sounds that letters make).

✏ **B1. Spelling My Name in Water -** Activity time: 30 minutes

Materials Needed
- One (1) clear glass or see-through plastic cup filled with pre-made blue Jell-O – set and ready to eat.
- One (1) 3x5 index card for each letter in the child's name
- One (1) black marker

Instructions:

Step 1: Using scissors, the adult should cut each 3x5 index card in half.

Step 2: Using a black marker, the adult should write the child's name, writing one letter on each index card. Make sure to use **Uppercase** and **Lowercase** letters.

Step 3: Repeat Step 2 on the other stack of index cards. After completing this step, you should have two sets of index cards, each set including the letters in the **child's first name**.

Step 4: Put one set of index cards on a table. The letters should be **in a random order.**

Step 5: Place the other set of index cards on the table **in the order the child's name is spelled**.

Step 6: Have the child hold the Jell-O cup. Tell them to look through the Jell-o to the bottom of the cup (the "water"). Tell them to place the cup over the letters that are mixed up.

When they look through the cup, say:

> **Adult:** "(Child's name), (child's name), what do you see?".
>   Have them responds with:
> **Child:** "I see the letter _____ in the deep blue sea."

Step 7: Tell the child to use a pen to copy the letters they see onto a blank piece of paper.

Step 8: Can the child organize the index cards into the order their name is spelled?

Step 9: Can the child rewrite the letters in the order their name is spelled?

Step 10: Time to eat the Jell-O!

Take it to the Next Level:

Repeat the activity using the child's last name.

B.1 Learning Objectives

Math/Science	Language/Literacy	Problem Solving	Motor Skills
•Discovery	•Vocabulary building • Imagination and Creativity •Name Identification •Alphabet Identification •Repetition •Phonological Awareness •Letter and Word Knowledge •Concepts of Print	• Imagination and Creativity •Matching •Socio-Dramatic Play •Comprehension of Meaning	•Fine Motor: Emerging Writing

Notes: What did your child do well? Are there any skills they need to continue to work on?

B2. Number Words: One through Five - Activity time: 15 minutes

Materials Needed
☐ One (1) Pen or Crayon
☐ Two (2) Blank pieces of paper

Instructions:

Step 1: On one piece of blank paper, write the following words:

One	Six
Two	Seven
Three	Eight
Four	Nine
Five	Ten

Step 2: Draw a line down the middle on the other piece of paper.

Step 3: Write half of the letters of the alphabet on one half of the paper and the other letters of the alphabet on the second half.

See example below:

A	N
B	O
C	P
D	Q
E	R
F	S
G	T
H	U
I	V
J	W
K	X
L	Y
M	Z

Step 3: Tell the child you're going on a word hunt. Tell them to look at the **number words** written on the paper from Step 1.

Step 4: Ask your child to use a crayon to draw one tally mark next to each letter they find on the paper from step 2. See the following example:

A			N	
B			O	
C			P	
D			Q	
E	I I I I	(4 E's)	R I I	(2 R's – from words "Three and Four"
F	I I	(2 F's)	S I I.	(2 S's – from words "Six and Seven"

Step 5: Ask your child to count the total number of tally marks next to each letter. Help them write the numeral next to the tallies.

See example below:

C   0
Zero C's in the number words.

P 0
Zero P's in the number words

D   0
Zero D's in the number words

Q 0
Zero Q's in the number words

E   I I I I   4
Four E's in the number words

R I I 2
Two R's in the number words

Step 6: Next, ask the child to count how many letters have **"0"** next to them.

Step 7: Repeat Step 5 asking them to count how many letters have the number **1** next to them.

Step 8: Repeat Step 6 for the numbers **two through ten**.

Step 9: Ask the child to use a highlighter to highlight the letters that have the most tally marks next to them.

B.2 Learning Objectives

Math/Science	Language/Literacy	Problem Solving	Motor Skills
• Number Identification • One to One Correspondence • Understanding Talley Marks • Using Numbers to Explain Quantity	• Vocabulary building • Alphabet Identification • Phonological Awareness • Letter and Word Knowledge • Concepts of Print • Introduction to Words and Number Symbols	• Matching • Categorizing • Letter Classification • Comprehension of Meaning	• Fine Motor: Emerging Writing

Notes: What did your child do well? Are there any skills they need to continue to work on?

B3. One to One Popsicle - Activity time: 25 minutes

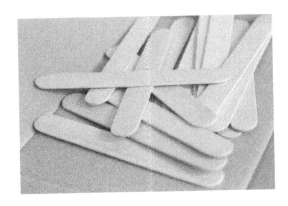

Materials Needed
- Fifty Five (55) Popsicle Sticks
- Ten (10) Plain White 3x5 Index Cards
- One (1) Pen
- One (1) Box of Crayons with the following colors: Brown, Blue, Red, Pink, Green, Purple
- One (1) set of Non-toxic, water proof paint with same colors as the Crayons
- One (6) Q-tips

Instructions:

Step 1: The adult should use a pen to write the **word "One"** on one of the blank 3x5 index cards.

Step 2: The adult should use a pen to write the **number "1" under the word "One"** on the same 3x5 index card.

Step 3: Repeat Step 1 and Step 2, writing the words "two" through "ten" AND the numbers 2 through 10 on the rest of the 3x5 index cards.

Step 4: Tell the child to listen to the following directions to make sure they use the correct colors.

Use the following key to tell the child which crayon color to use to trace the words on the index cards:

O words = **Blue Crayon**   F words = Green Crayon   E words = Brown Crayon
T words = Red Crayon   S words = **Purple Crayon**   N words = Pink Crayon

Example:

One	Two	Three	Four	Five
1	2	3	4	5

Step 5: The adult should place each 3x5 index card into a horizontal line.

One	Two	Three	Four	Five	Six	Seven	Eight	Nine	Ten
1	2	3	4	5	6	7	8	9	10

Step 6: Place **one Q-tip** into each of the paint colors (brown, blue, red, pink, green and purple).

Step 7: Tell your child to look at the numbers written on each 3x5 index card. Place the same amount of popsicle sticks, in a vertical line, underneath the matching 3x5 index cards.

See example below:

One 1	Two 2	Three 3	Four 4
I	I	I	I
	I	I	I
		I	I
			I

Step 8: Ask the child to name the color that each **number** is written in.

Step 9: Tell the child to look at the card with the number "Two" on it. The word "Two" is written with the color red.

Step 10: Tell the child to find the **Q-tip** that is in the red paint. Pick up that **Q-tip** and put two red dots on each popsicle stick **underneath the number "2" index card**.

See example below:

Two 2

| . |
.
.
.

Step 10: Repeat Step 9 for the rest of the index cards and popsicle sticks. Once completed, set the popsicle sticks aside to dry

---

Take it to the Next Level:

Allow child to use popsicle sticks and 3x5 index cards to repeat this activity throughout the week. Other ways to play the game include:

- o Match Popsicle sticks to the corresponding 3x5 index card
- o Place 3x5 index cards in order from least to most (1 to 10)
- o Place 3x5 index cards in order from most to least (10 to 1)

B.3 Learning Objectives

Math/Science	Language/Literacy	Problem Solving	Motor Skills
• Number Identification • One to One Correspondence • Understanding Tally Marks • Using Numbers to Explain Quantity	• Vocabulary building • Alphabet Identification • Phonological Awareness • Letter and Word Knowledge • Concepts of Print • Introduction to Words and Number Symbols	• Matching • Categorizing • Comprehension of Meaning • Color Identification	• Fine Motor: Emerging Writing

Notes: What did your child do well? Are there any skills they need to continue to work on?

B4. Shapely Letters - Activity time: 15 minutes

Materials Needed
☐ One (1) Piece of Blank Paper
☐ One (1) Pen
☐ One (1) Marker (any color)

Instructions:

Step 1: The adult should use a pen to draw the following shapes on a piece of blank paper.

- **Circle.**
- **Oval**
- **Square**
- **Rectangle**
- **Triangle**

Step 2: Ask the child to count how many sides are on a square.

Step 3: Tell the child to use a marker to write that numeral (number 4) in the middle of the square.

4

Note: Have them write the number **"0" for the Circle and the Oval since those shapes have **no sides.** See example below:

0

Step 4: Repeat Step 2 and 3 for all of the shapes.

Step 5: Help the child sound out the **first letter** of the **shape**.

> **Example:** "R" for rectangle. Can they make the **R** sound? Now have them repeat "rectangle".

Step 6: Have your child write the first letter that spells the shape next to each side of the shape. The amount of letters should equal the number that is written inside of the shape (**Note:** There will be no "C's" or "O's" written for Circle or Oval due to there being no sides).

See Example Below:

> **Rectangle:**
> There are four sides in a rectangle. Write the letter **"R"** next to each of the **four sides.** There are four R's!

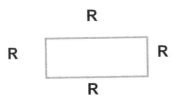

Step 7: Ask the child the following questions:
- Which shape has the most sides?
- Which shape has the least sides?
- Which shape has no sides?
- Are there two shapes that have the same amount of sides?

Take it to the Next Level:

Does the child know more shapes? Repeat Steps 1 through 5 with those shapes.

Shapes could include:
- Hexagon
- Diamond
- Octagon
- Any Others?

If the child is interested in shapes, teach them the names and images of shapes that have up to 10 sides.

B.4 Learning Objectives

Math/Science	Language/Literacy	Problem Solving	Motor Skills
• Number Identification • One to One Correspondence • Using Numbers to Explain Quantity • Shape Identification	• Vocabulary building • Alphabet Identification • Phonological Awareness • Letter and Word Knowledge • Description of Shapes	• Categorizing	• Fine Motor: Emerging Writing

Notes: What did your child do well? Are there any skills they need to continue to work on?

B5. Body Numbers - Activity time: 15 minutes

Materials Needed
- ☐ Two (2) Piece of Blank Piece of Construction Paper, Any Color
- ☐ One (1) Pen
- ☐ One (1) Box of Crayons or Markers

Instructions:

Step 1: Tell the child you're going to count from **one to ten!**

Step 2: Ask them to repeat the following phrase, filling in the amount they have of each body part:

"I have a lot of numbers all over me. I **have _(how many)__** fingers and I **have _(how many)__** toes. I **have _(how many)__** mouth and **_(how many)__** nose. I have **_(how many)__** eyes and **_(how many)__** ears. I have lots of numbers all over me."

Step 3: Tell the to repeat the following phrases. Have them point to each part of their body when named:

- I have _(how many)__ cheeks
- I have _(how many)__ chin
- I have _(how many)__ wrists
- I have _(how many)__ elbows
- I have _(how many)__ knuckles
- I have numbers all over me.
- I have _(how many)__ feet
- I have _(how many)__ hands
- I have _(how many)__ belly button
- I have _(how many)__ knees
- I have _(how many)__ ankles
- I have numbers all over me."

Step 4: Tell the child to use crayons to draw a picture of himself/herself on a blank piece of paper.

Step 5: Ask them to draw the same amount of body parts stated in Step 2 and Step 3. The adult should re-read each phrase.

Step 6: Once the child has drawn him/herself, tell the child to use a pen to write the number representing the quantity of each body part of the picture.

For example:
- Write "2" on each eye, hand, feed, knees, etc.
- Write "1" on the nose, belly button", etc.

B.5 Learning Objectives

Math/Science	Language/Literacy	Problem Solving	Motor Skills
• Number Identification • One to One Correspondence • Using Numbers to Explain Quantity	• Vocabulary building • Letter and Word Knowledge • Following Directions • Repeating Sentences • Use a Picture to Depict a Story	• Categorizing • Identifying Parts of the Body • Self Identification • Matching	• Fine Motor: Emerging Writing • Fine Motor: Drawing

Notes: What did your child do well? Are there any skills they need to continue to work on?

Gross Motor – Using our large muscles to move

By Completing Level 2 Activities, We will learn…

- o Uses gross motor movement skills to access a variety of obstacles and environments.
- o Hops on one foot, without support, three or more times.
- o Runs and Jumps over small objects.

Fine Motor – Using our hands to complete tasks

By Completing Level 2 Activities, We will learn…

- o Uses scissors appropriately.
- o Uses a crayon or pencil to draw or write.

C1. Side Shape Count - Activity time: 15 minutes

Materials Needed
- ☐ One (1) Piece of sidewalk chalk (or 1 roll of painters tape is completing activity inside)
- ☐ One (1) Measuring Tape
- ☐ Four (1) Pieces of Plain Paper
- ☐ One (1) Marker (Any color)

Instruction:

Step 1: Tell the child you're going to play a counting game.

Step 2: The adult should use sidewalk chalk (or painters tape) to make a 2-foot line for the child to stand behind. This will be the **"start"** line. (See Diagram in Step 4)

Step 3: The adult should use the measuring tape to measure **10 feet** away from the line in Step 2. (See Diagram in Step 4)

Step 4: The adult should use sidewalk chalk (or painters tape) to make another 2-foot line at the ten-foot mark in Step 3. This will be the **"finish"** line. See diagram below:

Start - - - - - - - - - - - - - - - -10 feet- - - - - - - - - - - - - - - - - - **Finish**

Step 5: Using a marker, the adult should draw **one circle** on one piece of blank paper.

Step 6: Using a marker, the adult should draw **one triangle** on one piece of blank paper.

Step 7: Using a marker, the adult should draw **one square** on one piece of blank paper.

Step 8: Using a marker, the adult should draw **one rectangle** on one piece of blank paper.

Step 9: Have the child **stand behind the "Start"** line.

Step 10: Hold up one piece of paper with one of the shapes on it.

> **Example:** Hold up the **picture of the square.**

Step 11: Ask the child **how many sides does the shape have?**
    Example: A Square has four sides.

Step 12: Tell the child to take that amount of steps towards the finish line.

    Example: One **square has four sides**, so that child can **take four steps** towards the finish line.

    Note: If a Circle or Oval is shown, they have **zero sides** so the child **doesn't take any steps.**

Step 13: Repeat step 8 through 11, holding up different shapes each time.

Step 14: Stop once the child reaches the finish line.

Step 15: Repeat step 9 through 13 as many times as you would like.

C.1 Learning Objectives

Math/Science	Language/Literacy	Problem Solving	Motor Skills
• Number Sense • One to One Correspondence	• Following Directions	• Association • Shape Identification • Numeral Identification	• Gross Motor: Walking • Gross Motor: Coordination

Notes: What did your child do well? Are there any skills they need to continue to work on?

C2. Patterned Numbers - Activity time: 15 minutes

Materials Needed
- ☐ Ten (10) Pieces of blue construction paper (cut up into equal pieces)
- ☐ Ten (10) Pieces of green construction paper (cut up into equal pieces)
- ☐ Two (1) Empty containers (large enough for the colored paper pieces to fit into)
- ☐ One (1) Black Marker
- ☐ An area where the child can move around

Instructions:

Step 1: The adult should write a single number (1 through 10) on the 10 pieces of blue construction paper. Write one number on each piece of paper.

Step 2: The adult should place the papers from Step 1 into one of the empty containers.

Step 3: The adult should write the following words (1 word per sheet) on the 10 pieces of green construction paper.

1. Jump
2. Hop
3. Walk
4. March
5. Tip Toe
6. Spin
7. Head Tap (touch head with hands)
8. Toe Tap (touch toes with hands)
9. Floor Touch (touch the floor with hands)
10. Body Wiggle (wiggle all around)

Step 4: The adult should place the paper from Step 3 into an empty container.

Step 5: Tell the child you're going to pull out one piece of green paper and one piece of blue paper. The green piece of paper is going to tell the child **what** to do and the blue piece of paper is going to tell the child **how many** to do.

Step 6: The adult should start by pulling one piece of blue paper **and** one piece of green paper out.

Step 7: Can the child identify what number you pulled out? The adult should read the action word on green paper.

See example below:

Green Paper   Blue Paper
Jump   7

Step 8: Ask the child to complete the direction. **(Example in Step 7: Jump seven times).**

Step 9: Repeat Step 6 through Step 7 three more times.

Step 10: Now tell the child that you are going to create a **"moving pattern."** The adult should pull out two green sheets of paper and two blue sheets of paper.

Step 11: The adult should place both pieces of green pieces of paper on the floor and place both pieces of blue paper on the floor.

Example:

Walk	3
Spin	7

Step 12: Ask the child to complete the directions (these are two-step unrelated directions).

> **To complete the example** in Step 11: The child should **walk for three steps** and then **spin in a circle seven times.**

Step 13: Tell the child that you are going to make the steps into a pattern. Repeat each pattern three times. Can they do it?

> **Example:** To complete the pattern from example from Step 11, the child would:
> 1. Walk 3 steps
> 2. Spin 7 times
> 3. Walk 3 steps
> 4. Spin 7 times
> 5. Walk 3 steps
> 6. Spin 7 times

Step 14: Repeat step 10 through Step 13 three times.

Take it to the Next Level:

Tell the child that you are going to add another action and number to the pattern to make a **three- step pattern.**

The adult should pick three green pieces of paper and three blue pieces of paper out of the containers. Place them in order and repeat step 10 through 12 using three steps.

See Example Below:

Walk	3
Spin	7
Jump	5

C.2 Learning Objectives

Math/Science	Language/Literacy	Problem Solving	Motor Skills
• Number Sense • One to One Correspondence • Counting 1 through 10	• Following two and three-step Directions	• Association • Number Identification • Color Identification • Following Visual Cues	• Gross Motor: Coordination • Gross Motor: Balance

Notes: What did your child do well? Are there any skills they need to continue to work on?

C3. Measurement Spoons - Activity time: 30 minutes

Materials Needed

- ☐ One piece of Sidewalk Chalk (or one roll of painters tape if choosing to do this activity indoors)
- ☐ Large Indoor or Outdoor Space
- ☐ Thirty (30) Plastic Spoons

Instructions:

Step 1: The adult should use sidewalk chalk to draw a **one-foot-long,** straight line, on the sidewalk.

Step 2: The adult should use sidewalk chalk to draw a **three-foot-long,** straight line, on the sidewalk.

Step 3: The adult should use sidewalk chalk to draw a **five-foot-long,** straight line, on the sidewalk.

Step 4: The adult should use sidewalk chalk to draw a **seven-foot-long,** straight line, on the sidewalk.

Step 5: Tell the child they're going to use plastic spoons to measure how long the lines are.

Step 6: Have the child place one plastic spoon at the edge of a line, covering the line from Step 1.

Step 7: Have the child place another plastic spoon, on the same line in Step 6.

Step 8: Have the child continue to place more plastic spoons above the previous plastic spoon until the line in Step 1 is **completely covered (in length)** with plastic spoons.

Step 9: Ask the child to count how **many spoons** it took to cover Line 1.

Step 10: Tell the child to use the chalk to write down the numeral that represents the number of plastic spoons from Step 9.

Step 11: Repeat step 6 through 10 will the other three lines.

Step 12: Once completed, ask the child to identify:
- Which line had that most spoons?
- Which line had the least amount of spoons?

Step 13: Can they identify the numbers they wrote on the ground?

C.3 Learning Objectives

Math/Science	Language/Literacy	Problem Solving	Motor Skills
• Number Sense • One to One Correspondence • Understanding Measurement • Demonstrating Size Comparison • Number Identification	• Following Directions • Understanding Big vs. Small	• Following Visual Cues	• Fine Motor: Writing Numbers

Notes: What did your child do well? Are there any skills they need to continue to work on?

C4. Scissor Snip - Activity time: 20 minutes

Materials Needed
- ☐ One pair of Child safe scissors
- ☐ Ten (10) pieces of same size paper (Any color)
- ☐ One (1) Marker

Instructions:

Step 1: The adult should use a marker to write the numbers "1" through "10", writing one number on each of the 10 pieces of paper.

Step 2: Place all ten pieces of paper in front of the child.

Step 3: Tell the child to use child safe scissors to "snip" each piece of paper. They should snip each piece of paper the same amount of times as the number written on it.

For example:

Numeral on paper	Amount of Snips with Scissors
1	1 snip
2	2 snips
3	3 snips

C.4 Learning Objectives

Math/Science	Language/Literacy	Problem Solving	Motor Skills
• One to One Correspondence • Number Identification	• Following Directions	• N/A	• Fine Motor: Using Scissors Appropriately

Notes: What did your child do well? Are there any skills they need to continue to work on?

C5. Number and Color Scramble - Activity time: 15 minutes

Materials Needed
- ☐ Ten (10) Pieces of Colored paper (each paper must be a different color)
- ☐ One (1) Black Marker
- ☐ Ten (10) Crayons (the crayons should be the same colors of the 10 pieces of construction paper).
- ☐ One (1) Empty Container

Instructions:

Step 1: The adult should use the marker to write the numbers "1" through "10" on the pieces of paper. Only write one number on each piece of paper.

Step 2: Place the pieces of the construction paper on the floor, either in a line or a circle.

Step 3: Place ten crayons (one crayon to match each color of construction paper) into an empty container.

Step 4: Tell the child you're going to pick out a crayon from the container. Whatever crayon color the adult picks out, the child must jump to the paper on the floor that's the same color.

Step 5: Once the is on the matching colored paper, ask them what number is written on that piece of paper.

Step 6: Tell the child to **jump** the amount of times that is written on the identified paper.

Step 7: Repeat steps 4 through 6 as many times as you would like.

C.5 Learning Objectives

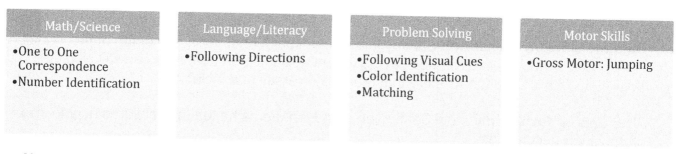

Math/Science	Language/Literacy	Problem Solving	Motor Skills
• One to One Correspondence • Number Identification	• Following Directions	• Following Visual Cues • Color Identification • Matching	• Gross Motor: Jumping

Notes: What did your child do well? Are there any skills they need to continue to work on?

Sammy the Golden Dog Series

The Playful Alphabet teaches letter sounds, formation and identification through play. By completing this books, children will be able to:

- Name and match Uppercase letters.
- Accurately write all Letters of the Alphabet.
- Demonstrate Phonological Awareness of every Letter (The sounds that letters make).

Sammy Chases the Alphabet: Play fetch with Sammy, the golden retriever, as he teaches your child all about the alphabet!

Sammy Goes to Preschool: Sammy joins his animal friends for a day of fun at preschool! He learns that although all his friends have different abilities then him, they can still all play together. This is a wonderful story that teaches diversity and inclusion.

The Search for Sammy: Join Sammy on an adventure as he teaches children how to stay safe if they ever become lost.

Soothing Sammy Program: This program teaches preschoolers how to calm down, communicate and problem solve in a positive way. This program is a great tool to teach social and emotional skills at home or in the classroom.

Find all of these resources and more at:
www.JDEducational.com

More Pre-K Your Way Activities:

LEVEL 1: SOCIAL EMOTIONAL SKILL CURRICULUM

**Note: This level is appropriate for children of all ages, regardless of academic level.

* Themed Academic Activities which use items found around the home to teach math, science, language, literacy, pre-writing skills to meet **Level 1 Learning Objectives are perfect for 2 year olds**.

* Behavior Support Tips & Worksheets - sections that provide ideas and strategies for parents which support age-appropriate social and emotional milestones.
These tips include helping their child Understand Diversity, Understand Safety Routines, Take Turns with Loved Ones and MORE!

LEVEL 2: INTERMEDIATE ACADEMIC CURRICULUM (ALPHABET AND MORE)

* Themed Academic Activities which use items found around the home to teach math, science, language, literacy, pre-writing skills to meet **Level 2 Learning Objectives, perfect for 3 year olds!**

Themes include: My Community, Roadways and Signs, Advanced Opposites, Space Exploration and MORE!

LEVEL 3: ADVANCED ACADEMIC CURRICULUM

* Themed Academic Activities which use items found around the home to teach math, science, language, literacy, pre-writing skills to meet **Level 3 Learning Objectives perfect for 4-6 year olds!**

Themes include: Camping, Transportation, Planet Earth, Construction, Oceanography and MORE!

* All Inclusive Academic Projects include all academic and social learning objectives. Each project guides the child to develop a hypothesis, research answers and form a conclusion. Projects include: Transportation: Understanding Package Delivery Systems, Project Weather: Discovering the Elements, Project Earth: Reduce, Reuse and Recycle, Project Construction: Building Components and Design and MORE!

About the Author

Jeana Kinne (maiden name Downey) has worked in a variety of positions in the Early Childhood Education field. While attending Sonoma State University (SSU), Kinne worked at the campus preschool where she became passionate about creating quality preschool environments and developing enriched play-based curriculum.

Kinne received a Bachelor's degree in Sociology and Human Development, followed by a Master's degree in Education: Curriculum, Teaching and Learning with an emphasis in Child Psychology. She has since held a variety of positions within the Child Development field – including Preschool Teacher, Preschool Director, Early Childhood Behavioral Specialist, Preschool Consultation Specialist, Parenting Education and Early Intervention Specialist (working with infants and toddlers with developmental delays). She is also a guest lecturer at the local Community college.

Through working with parents and other Early Childhood Education professionals, it became clear that a parent's engagement in their child's academic and social development is a key component to the child's continued success. Kinne created this Curriculum Series to provide parents with an opportunity to become actively engaged in their child's development, enhancing their school readiness skills.

Made in the USA
Coppell, TX
24 April 2022

76950757R10155